Gifted & anointed

THE LIFE OF THOSE WHO
EXHIBIT THE CHARACTER
OF THE MELCHIZEDEK
ANOINTING ORDER

OGHENETHOJA UMUTEME

Gifted & anointed

MEMOIRS

Cirencester

Published by Memoirs

MEMOIRS
P U B L I S H I N G

Memoirs Books

25 Market Place, Cirencester, Gloucestershire, GL7 2NX
info@memoirsbooks.co.uk www.memoirspublishing.com

Gifted and Anointed (c)Oghenethoja Umuteme, October 2012
First published in England, October 2012
Book jacket design Ray Lipscombe

ISBN 978-1-909304-47-5

Unless otherwise indicated, Bible quotations are taken from the King James Version of the
Holy Bible. Scripture quotations marked NIV are taken from the Holy Bible, New
International Version, copyright 1973, 1978, 1984 by the International Bible Society. Other
quotations marked ESV refers to the English Standard Version translation of the Holy Bible.

Address all enquiries to the publisher;
Restoration Media House Limited +234-8101700665, +2348076190064,
Email: rmhltd.info@gmail.com

Although the author and publisher have made every effort to ensure that the information in this
book was correct when going to press, we do not assume and hereby disclaim any liability to any
party for any loss, damage, or disruption caused by errors or omissions, whether such errors or
omissions result from negligence, accident, or any other cause.
The views expressed in this book are purely the author's.

Printed in England

CONTENTS

The time has come for mankind to take a journey that will unite us with the origin of all things, whence comes the breath of life. As it was in the days of old when no life existed in the womb of creation - when life existed without beginning and end, seen only through the far-reaching depth of the thoughts of El Elyon, who made all for His glory.

Oh Jehovah! Your mercies reach unfathomable depths of forgiveness. Use this book to reach the deepest of hearts and mould them in your potter's wheel, so that they may bless your name until that day when you draw the curtain to end this drama show on earth.

PROLOGUE

We are all gifted, being born for a purpose, but many of us have yet to discover that we can grow and develop better in our individual gifts through the anointing. Whatever gift you have, which has given you the ability to be talented in some specific things which you do with ease or in a career you are pursuing, the anointing is what beautifies it to the extent that it will be appreciated by people, and then you will blossom. This beautification process is your own responsibility (Matthew 5:16). This book is based on insightful revelations, and the information contained here may not be easily discerned by mere human wisdom. It is the result of my quest to know why many fail to succeed in life. The information in this book will help you understand the anointing, receive it and exercise it so as to become successful in life.

In this book we will see the anointed in two groups – one of those called and anointed to serve in the vineyard, whom we refer to as servants of God, and one of those who are not specifically called into pastoral ministry, but who need the anointing to excel in their individual careers on earth, so that they may blossom beyond human understanding. This group would be seen as those supporting the work and calling of God upon the servants of God, through whom they received the anointing, and would become their father in the Lord.

Also, as you read further, you are going to understand the reasons behind the extraordinary success experienced by someone anointed by God as compared to the ordinary man, in all areas of human endeavour. It is an insightful and revelation-packed teaching on the character of the Melchizedek Order.

The anointing is the arm of longevity from God. It is what takes us out of sin and links us to the glory of God, for all have sinned and come short of the glory of God (Romans 3:23). 'Touch not my Anointed' is the Lord's instruction in 1 Chronicles 16:22, and everyone who would want God's guardianship and leadership would sincerely and diligently seek to become anointed.

The anointing brings God's care and protection. Jesus was protected from Herod by the anointing upon Him. Moses was protected from Pharaoh because of the task ahead of Him, which He would do to deliver the children of God. The Bible confirmed this that there was glory ahead of Jesus and as such He had to endure the cross, implying that the anointing is an investment of God upon a man to enable his achievement on earth.

The anointing attracts the spirit of God. This is why Jesus says that we should only be afraid of He who can kill the Spirit. When the

Anointed is still a child, he needs protection until he is able to care for himself and understand the anointing he carries. Jesus had his parents to protect him. Moses had Miriam, and then his mother.

The Anointed is born with a sign, which becomes a mark upon him, which is not hidden. This links him to the Order all the time – the reason behind the star of Jesus which the wise men from the east saw. This sign indicates what kind of work the Anointed is to achieve on earth. The anointing is sometimes in your name and it spells your duty on earth as we would see in many of the Biblical names. This is why Herod wanted Jesus dead, because the Anointed is a threat to those in power who are ungodly. Great works come with the baptism of the Holy Ghost, enabling one to be on fire for the things of God, so that one can stand against evil practices. That is the whole essence of the anointing.

Jesus says: 'But ye shall receive power, after that the Holy Ghost is come upon you: and ye shall be witnesses unto me both in Jerusalem, and in all Judaea, and in Samaria, and unto the uttermost part of the earth.' (Acts 1:8). The anointing is for good works. Apart from your ability to do the work of God with zeal, the anointing, as I have seen in my own case as an engineer, will enable you to succeed even more in your chosen career in life, because the voice of the Lord will be leading you from behind whenever you are about to take a wrong decision: 'And thine ears shall hear a word behind thee, saying, This is the way, walk ye in it, when ye turn to the right hand, and when ye turn to the left' – Isaiah 30:21.

In order to commence work, the Anointed follows due processes which he receives from God. Jesus says He came to fulfil the law. This also include the training the Anointed must undergo to become perfect. Jesus had to listen to the teachers of the law at age twelve. Jesus says that it is the duty of the Anointed to fulfill all righteousness (Matthew 3:15).

The Anointed is announced by God: 'And lo a voice from heaven, saying, this is my beloved Son, in whom I am well pleased' (Matthew 3:17). It is like a matriculation and graduation ceremony. The matriculation is the calling. The graduation is the choosing – the Holy Ghost anointing, so that the Anointed can become zealous in performing the work he is anointed to carry out. As employees are promoted at work, so also the exploits of the Anointed earn him a reward from God. This is where your increase comes from. The exams we take in the university are like the temptations we go through, doing the work of God. Our recommendation by the Anointing Order comes from how many temptations we are able to overcome. This was why Jesus had to pass through the pain of death. God told me not to dodge temptations but to ask Him for wisdom to overcome them, because that is where announcement comes from as you learn daily. Indeed, Christ was led into the wilderness by the Spirit of God to be tempted by the devil (Matthew 4:1).

The Anointing admits you into a sub-Order of the Anointing Order and brings announcement, increase and establishment, as does the Melchizedek Order, which is the same yesterday, today and forever. As you read this book, desire to seek the anointing, work with it and abide by the rules that set it in place – the life of the Order, so that you will see increase and become established, because, you would become acquainted and live with the qualities of those qualified to stand before God in the tabernacle, outlined in Psalm 15 below:

Lord, who shall abide in thy tabernacle? who shall dwell in thy holy hill?

- *He that walketh uprightly, and worketh righteousness, and speaketh the truth in his heart.*
- *He that backbiteth not with his tongue, nor doeth evil to his neighbour, nor taketh up a reproach against his neighbour.*
- *In whose eyes a vile person is contemned; but he honoureth them that fear the Lord. He that sweareth to his own hurt, and changeth not.*
- *He that putteth not out his money to usury, nor taketh reward against the innocent. He that doeth these things shall never be moved.*

Life is not about noisy prayers or the expectation of miracles, but about adding value to the lives of those we meet daily – this is the essence of the love of God we share. And with the anointing you can do this onerous task of humanity better.

I wish you a wonderful exploration into the world of the Melchizedek Anointing Order.

Pst. Oghenethoja Umuteme
Royal Diamonds Int'l Church
(Christ Movement)
Port Harcourt
Nigeria

CHAPTER ONE

THE ANOINTING BASIS

God can do all things. He can turn a dumb man into an orator and a blind man into a prophet or seer. He can even turn a cripple into a high jumper. This He achieves through His anointing, as the Psalmist has to say in Psalm 89:20-21: *I have found David my servant; with my holy oil have I Anointed him: With whom my hand shall be established: mine arm also shall strengthen him.*

This strengthening arm is Jesus Christ, which is why King David says in Psalm 110:1-5: *'The Lord said unto my Lord, Sit thou at my right hand, until I make thine enemies thy footstool. The Lord shall send the rod of thy strength out of Zion: rule thou in the midst of thine enemies. Thy people shall be willing in the day of thy power, in the beauties of holiness from the womb of the morning: thou hast the dew of thy youth. The Lord hath sworn, and will not repent; Thou art a priest for ever after the order of Melchizedek. The Lord at thy right hand shall strike through kings in the day of his wrath.'* The reference to these verses in the

New Testament by Jesus and the Apostles – (Matthew 22:44, 26:64, Mark 12:36, Luke 20:42, Acts 2:34, 1 Corinthians 15:25, Hebrews 1:13, 5:6, 7:17, 21), only help to buttress this fact that Jesus, who sits at the right hand of God, is the Arm of the Lord.

The passage above says that the Lord shall send the rod of His strength out of mount Zion, where the Lord will rule in the midst of His enemies. What makes mount Zion unique? - *But ye are come unto mount Zion, and unto the city of the living God, the heavenly Jerusalem, and to an innumerable company of angels, To the general assembly and church of the firstborn, which are written in heaven, and to God the Judge of all, and to the spirits of just men made perfect* (Hebrews 12:22-23). The reggae icon Bob Marley once sang, 'Zion train is coming our way,' referring to the day of the Lord when He would judge the world. Mount Zion is the heavenly Jerusalem from which Jesus rules, as the rod of God's strength, resting upon His Arm, as a judge's rod of justice. When you are initiated into this Order and you begin to take root, these innumerable angels will stand to honour any command you give because the anointing makes you their judge (1 Corinthians 6:3), and your success in life will blossom for all to see, to the glory of God.

Why would you judge the angels? You are joint heirs with Christ and since you already have the mind of Christ, it means that whatever instructions you would give to them will not be worldly, and so if they disobey you, they have likewise disobeyed Jesus Christ, and then God the Father. We would see in Revelation 2 how Jesus judged the angel of the churches – He commended them where they did right and reprimanded them where they erred. Now this is where the angels would not forgive anybody who erred against them, who refused to carry out the instructions of the Order. Refusal to appreciate their help through thanksgiving unto God is not taken likely by them.

Don't forget that angels cook meals too, which they use to feed God's servants (1 Kings 19:5, 7). So when they intervene in your situation, they expect you to present a gift of appreciation which they would use to cater for the needs of the servant of God who they have found to be an intermediary between the spirit world and the physical. Without such a servant their duty will be onerous, as they will have to be transformed into humans every time they have information to give, as in the days of old. They take the lead to ensure you get to your destination daily, and that your days on earth are fulfilled (Exodus 23:20). We can only command angels when we are holy, because they are holy. This is the only reason why they would present your prayers before the throne of God (Revelations 8:3).

How do you command angels? Simple: 'Angels of the living God, meet Brother John and inform him I want to see

3

him at the church premises by 9 am tomorrow.' And when you see John, he will confirm that a voice spoke to him and told him to come over to see you. Angels only carry out holy instructions, so the prayer of a sinner is an abominable offence before the holy angels.

This brings the willingness to exercise the gift in us into our heart in the day of the power of the Lord, which is the anointing, judging from Psalm 89:20-21. This implies that anyone who wants to succeed in life must become connected to this power of God, who is also Jesus Christ – 1 Corinthians 1:24.

More and more, as the day grew, I could see the Arm of the Lord taking me higher than I ever expected, even while I was a baby in the things of the Lord before He arrested me by His spirit. This gives me more assurance that with God, all things really are possible. As scripture puts it: *But God hath chosen the foolish things of the world to confound the wise; and God hath chosen the weak things of the world to confound the things which are mighty; And base things of the world, and things which are despised, hath God chosen, yea, and things which are not, to bring to nought things that are: That no flesh should glory in his presence* - 1 Corinthians 1:27-29.

As I watched my wife, I could see this anointing being transferred daily without hesitation. Surely the Arm of the Lord is not too short to save. This book will explain how the Lord's anointing can help anyone to become successful in life, in any human endeavour of honour.

Books have already been written about anointing and what it is supposed to achieve. While I am not against the understanding offered by these books, it has become necessary to practicalise the purpose of the anointing in the lives of the children of God in such a way that they can relate to it in terms they can easily understand. The Hebrew word for 'anoint' is *mashach*, which is the root word for messiah - 'Anointed one.' This means that this book is all about how the power of the Lord and His wisdom can fill us, and help us to become willing with the ability to successfully carry our individual duties on earth in a perfect manner, in such a way that we please God.

St. Paul says in Philippians 4:13: *I can do all things through Christ who strengthens me.* This faithful saying is what this book will be asserting to reassure every one of us that the Arm of the Lord of old is very present in our midst, even to the end of time.

Now if we take a look at what God said in Genesis 2:5-6: *The earth was there but there was no vegetation because there was yet no rain and no man to till the earth, but there was a mist which watered the earth's surface – yet there was not vegetation.* What does this mean? The earth already received a gift of reproduction when it was formed out of the water and God speaking to it to bring forth vegetation (Genesis 1:9-10, 11). But it still had to depend on the rain from heaven and the availability of someone to till the ground.

Let us see the facts here as they relate to our gifts and how they would eventually become a point of attraction before men as a house set upon a mountain, the salt of the earth and a light that shines in darkness, with the thoughts of our hearts purer than diamonds and sparkling scintillatingly, so that God would eventually receive glory for our sake (Matthew 5:16). Everyone born on to the earth has a gift of fruitfulness in him/her, where lies the internal anointing, characterized by his/her spectacular behaviour, which is differentiated from those of other children.

This internal anointing is the 'main anointing', which is only acting as the mist and is unable to encourage vegetation or bear abiding fruits. Then the rain of God comes down, the supporting anointing, in the form of wisdom, to enable the internal anointing which has been producing the mist to overflow its bank, becoming rivers of living waters. And then the fruits will begin to blossom, and whatsoever he/she sows in that overflowing stream of water, representing doors of opportunities, referred to as the gifts of the spirit of God in the New Testament, will begin to burgeon. What he/she needs to do then is to tender it, obeying every command from God, else he/she will lose it to the devil's tricks.

First I would want to explain that anointing is not about someone shouting at the top of his voice and driving out demons, like the character of many who say they are possessed by the spirit of God. The anointing is like an admission into the Order of increase – the Order of God - and represents a letter of recommendation from God to enable Him to have someone who can interface with Him to bring information to His children to enable them 'learn to do well,' which is what God expects from man: *Learn to do well; -* Isaiah 1:17.

The anointing brings you into the 'relationship management' circle of God. Here you are in a circle of influence of the Order of righteousness. We can see this in His visit to the Garden of Eden that evening to ascertain the extent to which man was tendering the garden. If we don't receive instructions from Him, how can we know the things that have been freely given to us? Jesus told us that it is the will of God that we receive good from Him always when He said: *If ye then, being evil, know how to give good gifts unto your children, how much more shall your Father which is in heaven give good things to them that ask him?* (Luke 1:11). So we would say that the anointing is an avenue that enables God to recruit persons who now becomes His employees, assigned to do specific tasks in His vineyard: *For the kingdom of heaven is like unto a man that is an householder, which went out early in the morning to hire labourers into his vineyard.* (Matthew 20:1).

God communicates His heart's desires to us, just as the Managing Director of a company would want to cascade management decisions down the leadership hierarchy. This is why in Isaiah 1:18 He says: *Come now, and let us reason together, saith the Lord...* The purpose of the anointing is seen from this premise as a letter of engagement in the service of the supernatural Order of God.

To drill down further to discover what the anointing process entails, we would have to listen to Jesus' words of invitation in Matthew 11:28-30: *Come unto me, all ye that labour and are heavy laden, and I will give you rest. Take my yoke upon you, and learn of me; for I am meek and lowly in heart: and ye shall find rest unto your souls. For my yoke is easy, and my burden is light.* From here we could see that:

- God is admitting and recruiting people into this Anointing Order - *Come unto me.*
- The recruitment process involves invitation. Jesus' announcement of admission and employment chances is proclaimed in public just as schools and organizations would advertise in the mass media.
- The category of those expected is also explained - *that labour and are heavy laden.*
- The earnest expectation of God is seen in the first verse also - *I will give you rest.*
- What happens in the Anointing Order for God to fulfill His own part of the agreement is explained to include two

processes: Receiving the anointing upon Him - *Take my yoke upon you,* and the process of indoctrination and enculturation - *and learn of me.*

■ He went further to explain the details of the Anointing Character - *for I am meek and lowly in heart.*

■ Then He explains in simple terms the dynamic nature of the work the Anointed will be doing as he/she matures - *For my yoke is easy, and my burden is light.* There is a yoke – duty call, and that yoke will bear a burden – tasks to accomplish with the anointing. This is why Romans 8:28 says: ... *to them who are the called according to his purpose.* And in 1 Corinthians 7:20 the Bible instructed: ... *Let every man abide in the same calling wherein he was called.* Sometimes this requires perseverance from the Anointed that have to bear the pain of service. As can be seen in the Levites who stayed in the middle of the river Jordan until the entire nation of Israel had crossed – Joshua 3:17. This is typical of the Levitical Order responsibilities – readiness to bear the burden of the Lord (Ezra 3:9). Another instance would be when the hand of Moses must not come down, but continually stretched to heaven – Exodus 10:22.

The burden borne by the Anointed, who minister before the Lord, is the reason the Order wants them to be properly taken care of by those they minister to, who then becomes linked to the Order for protection and blessings. We see an instance of this in Ezekiel 4:5-6: *I have assigned you the same number of days as the years of their sin. So for 390 days you will bear the sin of the house of Israel. 'After you have finished this, lie down again, this time on your right side, and bear the sin of the house of Judah. I have assigned you 40 days, a day for each year-*(NIV).

The Spirit of God in us unites us to have a common purpose and then we would be able to obey the commands of the Order: *I will give them an undivided heart and put a new spirit in them; I will remove from them their heart of stone and give them a heart of flesh. Then they will follow my decrees and be careful to keep my laws. They will be my people, and I will be their God –* Ezekiel 11:19-20 (NIV). This common purpose is exemplified in the institution of the Holy Communion bread and wine, by the Order so that we would agree as one, living in the peace of God. Not until believers are able to unite will they see the manifestation of the Holy Communion in their lives. Many people take communion without knowing that it is a testimony on its own, just like the manna, and the rod of Aaron, which budded, and were kept in the Ark of the testimony of the Lord. Those who heard Jesus spoke about it in John 6:60-66 did walk out of Him because they knew the importance He attached to the communion service. It is a practice that reactivates the beauty of the Salvation Order. When this happens, anyone linked to the Order would sing like King David in Psalm 108:1 - *My heart, O God, is steadfast.* This is the confidence we have in Jesus as our firm foundation. The Bible says in 2 Timothy 2:19: *But God's firm foundation stands, bearing this seal: 'The Lord knows those who are his,' ...* This seal is the authority the Order hands down to whoever subscribes to and is initiated into the Order. The Holy Spirit confirms this seal when He comes upon the Anointed.

You may decide to use any physical object, which is with you as the possessing arm of the Order – Moses used his staff, Elijah used his mantle, Paul used his handkerchief. Elisha's bones was still bearing the Order's arm even in the grave, the devil wanted Moses dead body because it carries the Order's arm of authority so as to use it for his purpose, where Jesus' body had been lying was safeguarded by two angels during his transition into the deep – where He set lose those held bound by the devil – these two angels appeared to Mary – John 20:12.

■ We would see that the anointing is about admission to learn, employment to serve, and then qualification for reward from God to enable us find rest for our souls: *ye shall find rest unto your souls.*

The following are the facts about the Anointing:
1. The Anointing bearer and confirmer is the Holy Spirit.
2. The Anointing character is the personality of the Holy Spirit.

3. The Anointing leads to possession by the Spirit of God, which then come upon the recipient.

4. The Anointing initiates one into the Order of Melchizedek - the realm of immortality, where Christ exists and belongs.

5. The Anointing medium – olive oil, laying of hands, imbibing the word of God, etc, earmarks one who harkens to the voice of God for possession.

6. Once the Holy Spirit possesses one, God then takes over the mortal body, becoming His temple or dwelling place, making it easy for God to sanctify the body and then consecrate it for His use – Psalm 51:7: *Cleanse me with hyssop, and I will be clean; wash me, and I will be whiter than snow.* To be whiter than snow is to be pure in heart. And the pure in heart shall see God (Matthew 5:8).

7. Then the Anointed will begin to function in position – Romans 8:28.

8. The Anointing character enables the one Anointed to seek God and become possessed to act in the Order. The Angels can then minister to the Anointed. There are stages in the sanctification process – 1) Anointed; earmarking for Holy Spirit possession, and 2) Possession; earmarking for the ministration of Angels.

The Holy Spirit can be attracted into our lives by:

1. The Anointing oil from a servant of God: Saul and David were anointed by Samuel (1 Samuel 10:1, 16:13).

2. Laying of hands upon our forehead by a servant of God: Joshua received the spirit of wisdom through Moses (Deuteronomy 34:9).

3. Through Prayer: Ananias prayed for Saul (Paul) – Acts 9.

4. Through the sprinkling of water by a servant of God: Ezekiel 36:25-27.

5. During water Baptism – The Holy spirit descended on Jesus during His baptism (Matthew 3:16).

6. Through Breathing upon the person by an anointed servant of God learning from Jesus who breathed upon His disciples and commanded them to receive the Holy Spirit (John 20:22).

7. Through the meditational study of the word of God – the spirit of knowledge and understanding comes to give you insight (2 Timothy 2:15).

8. Through hearing and believing the word of God (Acts 10:44).

Once the Holy Spirit is done with His work of sanctification, the angels move into action to minister unto the Anointed and then present his prayers unto God. An instance would be the conception of Jesus; once Mary was pregnant with the Holy Spirit, Angel Gabriel visited her to let her know she was carrying the seed of the Order who will bruise the head of the serpent.

The moment God breathed into Adam he became a living soul. The moment the Holy Spirit sanctified the deformed earth, God's word took effect. This is the Anointing character. It prepares the environment for God's word to takes effect in our lives. I would liken the anointing character to a medical doctor living inside, in thoughts and action, the body of someone who is illiterate. This will automatically turned the person into one having the wisdom of medicine. The anointing therefore means that one is:

■ **Called to serve** – As Jesus' parable of the idle labourers pointed out, no one is expected to be idle in His house.

■ **Equipped to serve** – Jesus taught His disciples for three years.

■ **Certified to serve** – The event in Acts 2 shows that the Holy Spirit had certified them to serve in the Lord's vineyard.

■ **Commissioned to serve** – In Matthew 28:19-20, the great commission was instituted by Jesus, showing that the Anointed is detailed to serve as one in the military.

The Anointed raises disciples to work with him, making him more of a leader by anointing them. Some of these would be with him full-time like the twelve disciples, and others would still be in their professional careers, making a living and supporting the works of the ministry of Christ, but the anointing will make them exceptional in whatever they are doing. He/she values division of labour: Moses cried that God should give him who will work with him (Exodus 33:12).

The anointing comes in different stages which I have classified in two main categories as 'main anointing' and 'supporting anointing'. The main anointing is your destiny, which spells out what God has prepared you for from the womb, which is sometimes represented by the name you bear. The supporting anointing only makes the main anointing start working. The supporting anointing activates the main anointing so that it can be employed as a service to others. 'The greatest among you shall serve...' is a statement from Jesus showing that the Anointed receives the spirit of service to God and humanity the moment the main anointing is activated.

Service is the fire that burns the main anointing. Challenges also help to mature it. The learning you will encounter is related to your heart desire as you serve. If the learning is not in tune with the purpose of the main anointing, there will be a delay in achieving the purpose of the main anointing.

As we leave this chapter we must hold on to the following salient facts about the anointing:

- The Anointing is for work. The Anointed becomes God's tool.

- The anointing distinguishes one to serve in different capacities.

- The spirit of the Lord comes in once there is the mark of the anointing upon anyone.

- The anointing is the strength of God that makes us able to do the will of God. 'Let your will be done on earth as it is in heaven' is our earnest prayer, and the Anointed is the instrument God will use to cause this to happen. It brings one into the light of God. There was no chaos in heaven on the day of creation, so the moment we receive God through the anointing we will stop experiencing chaos.

- Anointing depicts a connection in place between God and His Anointed, making you do exactly what God wants you to do, as Jesus did when He confirmed that whatsoever God did that also He does. This implies that we must learn to know God more, daily.

- The anointing brings wisdom, since it unites you with the purpose of heaven, the Order of Melchizedek.

- The anointing is the arm of God, making you fully represent God here on earth. We must therefore see this teaching from the personality of God.

- The anointing brings about success in life, as could be seen in the lives and the acts of those who were under the anointing in the Bible.

- The anointing leads to one been filled with the gifts of the Holy Spirit. From the gifts of the Holy Spirit, the task of man is apportioned by the Order.

- The Anointed is a conqueror: Abraham was a mighty man in battle.

- The anointing brings influence - who was Elisha that the shunammite woman would accord such an honour, even when she was from a home of affluence, if not for the sake of the anointing?

- The Anointed is an inventor.

- He is an intelligent teacher.

- He is a Prophet of God to the nation.

- The Anointed is excellent in judgment, making him one with wise counsel.

CHAPTER TWO

THE ANOINTING ORDER

To buttress what we discussed in chapter one, the anointing is likened to an admission letter, qualifying you to be gainfully employed to serve in the Melchizedek Order. In schools we have classes of learning and one has to take exams to climb the ladder of academic learning. In an organisation, one is usually employed at a level that defines his/her obligations and as time goes on, he/she is appraised and promoted to take higher responsibilities with increased reward. This is what the anointing is all about – we must receive the anointing, and then grow into maturity in the things of the spirit. It is our maturity that defines our rewards: *For when for the time ye ought to be teachers, ye have need that one teach you again which be the first principles of the oracles of God; and are become such as have need of milk, and not of strong meat. –* Hebrews 5:12.

The Order requires one to pass through the process of Recruitment, Training and Spiritual Empowerment, so that you will be filled with the wisdom to enable you to execute the will of God on earth. These three stages could be said to imply Harvest, Recruitment and Preservation – training and spiritual empowerment. This premise will enable us to understand better what we shall be discussing in this chapter.

It is of importance to note that the main reason we are in this discussion is to overcome the devil's manipulation. One of the fragments of the Dead Sea scrolls made mention of Melchiresha as the king of evil. Fragment 4Q280 describes a series of curses laid upon Melchiresha: '*Accursed are you, Melchiresha, in all the plans of your guilty inclination. May God [make you] an object of dread at the hand of those exacting vengeance. May God not favour you when you call on him. [May he lift his angry face] upon you for a curse. May there be no peace for you in the mouth of those who intercede. [Be cursed,] without a remnant; and be damned, without salvation.*' – 4Q280.

Everyone possessed by the devil is initiated into the order of Melchiresha. The opposite of this order is Melchizedek – 'Priest of the Most High God'. The language spoken by the initiates is purely spiritual. This is what King David referred to as: *Deep calleth unto deep at the noise of thy waterspouts: all thy waves and thy billows are gone over me.* (Psalms 42:7). The feeling is more of a comforting experience. It is like someone who is very thirsty drawing water from a deep well, yet with the water filled to the surface. Hence the Holy Spirit is called the human comforter. This is why it requires your spiritual alertness and mental balance to be able to hear and act in accordance to the dictates of the Order.

In Psalms 110:4 we came to the understanding that there is an order where God initiates His elect into: *The Lord hath sworn, and will not repent, Thou art a priest for ever after the order of Melchizedek.* And in the book of Hebrews 5:5-6 it was explained that Jesus is indeed a King after this Order of righteousness: *So also Christ glorified not himself to be made an high priest; but he that said unto him, Thou art my Son, today have I begotten thee. As he saith also in another place, Thou art a priest for ever after the order of Melchizedek.* It is a fact that we are of a Royal Priesthood Order once we are in Christ. And since Jesus is the same today, yesterday and forever (Hebrews 13:8), we would say that the same old anointing that God instituted is still present in our present dispensation. Our God never changes – He is the 'I am that I am'. We are going to have a deeper understanding of this from the following Bible verses:

■ There is an anointing order called the Order of Melchizedek – Hebrews 7:1-3: *This Melchizedek was king of Salem and priest of God Most High. He met Abraham returning from the defeat of the kings and blessed him, and Abraham gave him a tenth of everything. First, the name Melchizedek means 'king of righteousness'; then also, 'king of Salem' means 'king of peace'. Without father or mother, without genealogy, without beginning of days or end of life, resembling the Son of God, he remains a priest forever* (NIV). This Order connects one to the vine of justification, sanctification, and consecration which forms the totality of righteousness. This true vine is mentioned as the tree of life in the Garden of Eden.

■ The Psalmist knew that this Order would bring the much expected peace in the land of Israel in Psalm 110:3: *Thy people shall be willing in the day of thy power, in the beauties of holiness …*

■ Jesus is affirmed the Anointed King who is the overseer of the Order, through a process known as 'begetting' - Hebrews 5:5-6. To beget is to anoint. And verse 6 concludes that He is a High Priest. This is why in Psalms 89:19-20 God says He found and then anoints one into the Order who would become mighty.

■ Anyone who obeys Him and is Anointed functions in this Order: *And being made perfect, he became the author of eternal salvation unto all them that obey him; Called of God an high priest after the order of Melchizedek.* (Hebrews 5:9-10).

■ This Order is the custodian of the mysteries and secret things of the Lord – Deuteronomy 29:29, 1 Corinthians 2:7-8. This is also confirmed in Hebrews 5:11: *Of whom we have many things to say, and hard to be uttered, seeing ye are dull of hearing.* The key statement here is - *hard to be uttered.* St Paul further called these secrets strong meat: *But strong meat belongeth to them that are of full age, even those who by reason of use have their senses exercised to discern both good and evil.* Another verse that explains this is 2 Corinthians 12:4: *How that he was caught up into paradise, and heard unspeakable words, which it is not lawful for a man to utter.* These mysteries establish the foundation of spiritual intelligence. One of such secrets is the Holy Communion. Earlier in chapter one, we learnt that the anointing attracts the Holy Spirit and the Holy Spirit attracts the angels of God to come and minister unto whoever is Anointed – this is a mystery, because they are beyond the wisdom of this physical Order.

■ Our souls as believers are tied unto this Order of righteousness, from whence we are monitored, controlled and our footsteps ordered as the King desires: *We have this hope as an anchor for the soul, firm and secure. It enters the inner sanctuary behind the curtain, where our forerunner, Jesus, has entered on our behalf. He has become a high priest forever, in the order of Melchizedek (NIV)* – Hebrews 6:19-20. This is what happened when Jesus was led into the wilderness to be tempted of the devil - Matthew 4:1: *Then was Jesus led up of the spirit into the wilderness to be tempted of the devil.*

■ Anyone who belongs to this Order is drawn near unto God and will never lack anything in life. This is why King

David prayed: *Restore to me the joy of your salvation and grant me a willing spirit, to sustain me.* – Psalm 51:12 (NIV). Jesus makes provisions for their needs so that they would function as priests of righteousness, Hebrews 7:26-28: *Such a high priest truly meets our need – one who is holy, blameless, pure, set apart from sinners, exalted above the heavens. ... He sacrificed for their sins once for all when he offered himself. For the law appoints as high priests men in all their weakness; but the oath, which came after the law, appointed the Son, who has been made perfect for ever.*

■ Anyone initiated into this order rides on a glorious donkey of announcement because anyone Anointed now, has been in Christ since the foundation of the earth. Inasmuch as Jesus rode on that donkey of announcement, and judging from Hebrews 7: 9-10 that Levi paid tithe because Abraham had paid tithe to Melchizedek, it would be right to say that whatsoever Jesus had accomplished while on earth is a demonstration of what the Melchizedek Order represents. This is why anyone called and chosen by God to be a bearer of the torch of salvation is announced abroad as a result of the manifestation of the secrets of the Order in his/her life.

The 'Anointing character' is the manifested attributes of anyone initiated into this order. These manifested attributes are seen in their quietness, meditation, compassion, tender eyes, steadfastness, and all round success, as the Order does not accept failure. The Order operates in 100% obedience to the will of God. This is why Prophet Samuel informed us about the law of the Order: *'Does the Lord delight in burnt offerings and sacrifices as much as in obeying the voice of the Lord? To obey is better than sacrifice, and to heed is better than the fat of rams.* – 1 Samuel 15:22. And again we would see Jesus surrendering to the will of the Order – Luke 22:42: *'Father, if you are willing, take this cup from me; yet not my will, but yours be done.'* (NIV).

The problem many of us have is that, after we have given our life to the Order, so that the Order will take charge over our existence on earth in protection and provision, we refuse to obey the Order's instructions. This disobedience is not usually overlooked by the angels who are actually sent from the Order to minister unto us - Exodus 23:20-21: *Behold, I send an Angel before thee, to keep thee in the way, and to bring thee into the place which I have prepared. Beware of him, and obey his voice, provoke him not; for he will not pardon your transgressions: for my name is in him.* This was why God referred to the Israelites as stiff necked people when they disobeyed Him – Exodus 32:9-10 (NIV): *'I have seen these people,'* the Lord said to Moses, *'and they are a stiff-necked people. Now leave me alone so that my anger may burn against them and that I may destroy them. Then I will make you into a great nation.'*

And we all know that when someone tries to bend a stiff neck, pain is usually inflicted. This is what happens when we refuse to follow the dictates of the Melchizedek Order, and as the angel tries to lead us through this unknown paths, except we are obedient, we won't walk far before we give up, and we would see ourselves suffering from the punishment of disobedience.

St. Paul opens our understanding to the requirement to become initiated into the Melchizedek Order – the Kingdom of Light when he says: *And we pray this in order that you may live a life worthy of the Lord and may please him in every way: bearing fruit in every good work, growing in the knowledge of God, being strengthened with all power according to his glorious might so that you may have great endurance and patience, and joyfully giving thanks to the Father, who has qualified you to share in the inheritance of the saints in the KINGDOM OF LIGHT [Melchizedek Order].–* Colossians 1: 10-12 (NIV) *Emphasis mine.*

Once a person is initiated into the Order, he/she moves into the stage of intimation and then implantation for the purpose of spiritual maturity through a process of inner spiritual awakening. These stages are what I refer to in my book, the path to absolute freedom as, the 'Triple-I model' – Initiation, Intimation and Implantation. For the purpose of clarity and not to keep the reader in suspense, these stages will be explained below.

The Melchizedek Order Initiation cycle

The Bible says: *Whosoever shall call on the name of God shall be delivered,* Joel 2:32, Acts 2:21. Therefore, call upon the name of God and be initiated into the realm of absolute freedom. Don't proceed until you have completed this Freedom Initiation Cycle (FIC). The Initiation Cycle (IC) is made up of a collection of words which will enable you move towards the Altar of God. You can actually start from the door facing the church altar, preferably dressed in white. Ensure you have taken a bath, and have your forehead Anointed, with olive oil.

The first cycle involves making the pronouncement: *Holy! Holy! Is the Lord God Almighty who reigns forever more.* Then you should wait for some minutes, to allow the living words which you just pronounced to resonate in your inner mind. After this, proceed further, just as Jesus did when He was praying in the garden of Gethsemane. With your hands gripped together into a fist, look directly into the Altar and ensure that you can see Jesus nailed on the cross. Once you can see Him now hanged on that cross, make the following pronouncement: 'Lord Jesus, save me from condemnation. I believe that truly You were hanged on the cross for my sake.' At this point, you should be remorseful for all the sins which you have committed. Thereafter, make the following pronouncement: 'I am sorry for all the sins which I have committed.' Visualize Him spreading out His hands to welcome you. Then say: 'Have mercy upon my soul!'

After that, it is proper to call upon the name Jesus; do this seven times. On the completion of the seventh cycle calling the name of Jesus, kneel in front of the Altar and pray.

Congratulations! You have been initiated into the Order of Melchizedek. Wait to be Anointed with the anointing oil before you leave. The man of God in the altar will be glad to do this.

The word of God says: *For then will I turn to the people a pure language that they may all call upon the name of God, to serve him with one consent.* Zephaniah 3:9.

Only the initiated can speak a pure language, an undaunted language, in their communications with God. Sin infuriates God. The above initiation practice cleanses us before God, and we are on our way to enjoying absolute freedom. Shalom!

The Triple-I Model

The Triple-I model helps us to know which stage we are in the Order as we mature into immortality in our thoughts. As we grow this ladder of maturity, we begin to hear what the spirit says. The main purpose of the growth is to attract the possession by the Holy Spirit, who is the officer who confirms whoever is accepted in the Order. Once we are confirmed by the Holy Spirit we start transiting from the mortal realm into immortal realm where we would be able to judge all things - 1 Corinthians 2:14-15: *The person without the Spirit does not accept the things that come from the Spirit of God but considers them foolishness, and cannot understand them because they are discerned only through the Spirit. The person with the Spirit makes judgments about all things, but such a person is not subject to merely human judgments* (NIV). The disciples quickly baptized those whom the Holy ghost fell on in Acts 10:44-48: *While Peter yet spake these words, the Holy Ghost fell on all them which heard the word. And they of the circumcision which believed were astonished, as many as came with Peter, because that on the Gentiles also was poured out the gift of the Holy Ghost. For they heard them speak with tongues, and magnify God. Then answered Peter, Can any man forbid water, that these should not be baptized, which have received the Holy Ghost as well as we? And he commanded them to be baptized in the name of the Lord.* The key to receiving the confirmation note in the Order is tied to the level of desire we have, which is referred to as FAITH. Below are the stages outlined in the Triple-I model.

- **Initiation Stage:** To be initiated into the Order, a process of forgiveness has to take place from God: *Hide your face from my sins and blot out all my iniquity* – Psalm 51:9 (NIV). But for God to do this we must forgive those who had wronged us (Matthew 6:12). At the Initiation stage, the believer is new to the faith, and trying to find his/her feet. He/she is probably attending the new believers' training session and getting indoctrinated in the rules of the Kingdom of God. Many at this point show regrets over the sins they have committed as the Holy Spirit ministered emotionally to their hearts, and the church provides Bibles for them. Here they are being followed up through a process we refer to as Knowing. He/she is also learning and undergoing the process of being born again. Many believers who refuse to grow after this stage become very religious, as is the case with many Church members. This stage is what Christ referred to as 'enter into life' (Matthew 19:17. St Paul referred to those in this stage as being justified by faith. Prior to this stage of spiritual awareness, we had all come short of the glory of God (Romans 3:23), because of the Adamic nature which we bore, before accepting Christ into our lives.

- **Intimation Stage**: The Intimation stage involves sanctification with the Word, as espoused by Jesus in John 17:17. The new believer obviously would be undergoing a deep reflective study of the Bible, a series of fasting and prayers and meditational silence. At this stage, the old sinful skin is being dropped and the believer is gaining more knowledge and understanding of God. He/she ought

by now to be in the advanced stage of the believers'
training class (school of ministry), and gradually taking up
roles in the local church of worship. The presence of the
Holy Spirit in the life of the new believer is conspicuous
and manifested through the crying out of the spirit of
Christ in their hearts, Galatians 4:6. During this stage, our
conscience comes alive more than ever before. The new
believer starts to understand the doctrine of the Christian
faith. The soul winner invests time and resources to ensure
the newly recruited is rooted in the faith. The church at
this stage organises training sessions aimed at making
him/her to receive the new birth in water and in the spirit,
which ushers the new convert into the kingdom of God
(John 3:5). The new convert focuses on Jesus more daily,
and he/she is committed to the extent that he/she can
leave every other engagement for the sake of the kingdom
(Matthew 19:21).

■ **Implantation Stage:** Once we have been approved by God,
having understood the purpose of God's kingdom through
a deep revelation, as espoused in 2 Timothy 2:15, we can
now become implanted. This portion of the Bible
says:...*study to show thyself approved unto God...* Thus, we
need to be consecrated and approved of God, which is the
basic ritual in the implantation stage. Jesus Christ begged
the father for a release of the Holy Spirit upon the

disciples, because without the infilling of the Holy Spirit, consecration cannot be achieved. This process, leading to consecration, clearly took the disciples three good years, listening to Jesus and doing His command, to achieve. But before this they had been sanctified, as indicated in John 17:17. This is the basis on which I made mention of a revelation-filled study. Although, in John 15:3 Jesus recommends that they had been clean because of the word which they had received, He still went further to breath the Holy Spirit upon them (John 20:22), before the outpouring in Acts 2 took place. The process of implantation is for the purpose of fruit bearing (John 15:5). This is to say that after you have been successfully implanted, through your act of bearing abiding fruits (John 15:16), you can now be found among those who are ready for heaven (Luke 12:37). As in the other stages, the spiritual path here is Consecration, meaning someone set apart for service unto God.

Once one is in the last stage of the Triple-I model, he/she becomes the Anointed. This is what is referred to as ordination. But I have seen that ordination as practice in many circles is more of a social exercise and not because those involved really know what they are doing. The ordination process is actually a process that only the Holy Spirit will confirm to have been done in line with the tenets of the Order: *For there is one God, and one mediator between God and men, the man Christ Jesus; who gave himself a ransom for all, to be testified in due time. Whereunto I am ordained a preacher, and an apostle, (I speak the truth in Christ, and lie not;) a teacher of the Gentiles in faith and verity.* - 1 Timothy 2:5-7. The word in this verse that speaks of the purpose of the ordination and why it is done is: *Whereunto I am ordained...* And as long as it is properly done because the Order has approved the ordained, he will become an instrument of peace – Matthew 5:9. No man can function as a Justice of Peace until approved by the Order: *Study to shew thyself approved unto God, a workman that needeth not to be ashamed, rightly dividing the word of truth.* – 2 Timothy 2:15.

We would now explain the Order character through the known – and we would be using the names of God in the Bible. A look at the names of God, both the ones He pronounced Himself and those ascribed to Him as a result of what He did in the lives of His chosen ones, we would be able to understand the character of the Order as follows:

■ **Resolute in decisions and actions:** The Order does things in a patterned and organised manner. The Order personalities remain steadfast, doing the same thing over and over again with clarity of purpose and intention. This would be seen in God declaring that His name is 'I am that I am.' The Order operates with a set standard of principles which points to righteousness and expects everyone on earth to live by that set standard. And this explains why He is called 'Jehovah Tsidkenu – Jeremiah 23:6,' unlike the devil, whose decision and actions are neither here nor there as he moves to and fro, without any concrete plan at heart but to ensure that every good intention in man fails and encouraging the wicked who has his seed at heart to perpetuate evil wherever they found themselves.

■ **Restoration:** The Order's interest would be summarized as the act of restoration. This is why God is referred to as 'Jehovah Rapha.' He heals. That is all that gives the Order joy. This is why we expect so many blessings from the Order. We see the Order as the embodiment of perfection and therefore anyone who subscribes to it would become perfect in thoughts, health and life. A look into Isaiah 42:22 would explain better the character of the Order – restoring all mankind had lost due to disobedience when we repent and display attitudes that show allegiance to the character of God. In order to achieve this restoration character, the Order goes into battles with the opposition – the devil, freeing the oppressed form his grip. An act that earns God the following names – Elohim, Ebenezer, Sabbaoth, and El Elyon.

■ **Purity:** The Order abhors stains and dirtiness. A look at the sky would explain this – the suns shines with clean, defined rays of light. There is a process of recycling and cleansing even in the human system. This is why anyone connected to the Order can never appreciate dirtiness. God is referred to as Maccaddeshem – Exodus 31:13, because He is a sanctifying God. This sanctifying attribute of the Order was what Jesus also referred to in John 17:17: *Sanctify them through thy truth: thy word is truth.* Apart from the natural cycles of purification that has been instituted by the Order, the world is illuminated with words spoken from the Order so that humans would be able to exhibit the character of the Order which spells truth. The more we hear the truths concerning our situations and know the answers to our questions of insatiable physical and spiritual quests, the more we become freed.

■ **Vision:** God sees the end from the beginning. We can even have a little understanding of this from the power of vision of birds of prey like the kite and the eagle. This is physical seeing and the reason why He has given eyes to humans and animals alike.

The Order sees and can distinguish darkness from light, different colours and beauty. The beauty in flowers and the colours seen throughout the world exist because of the expectation and aspiration of the Order. Anyone possessed by the Order's spirit lives a life of vision and the appreciation of beauty. This is why in Exodus 31:1 the Order had to select someone who appreciates the beauty of skilful entrepreneurship to build God's tabernacle. God is El Roi because He sees. This is the character that made the Order appreciate what God created in Genesis 1, and they were acclaimed as good and then, very good. Someone who sees would know where to make changes so that the beauty would possess the power of attraction. This is why the devil also walks in our sight and shows us beauty which we would appreciate before he would lead us from the path of God, because vision is a spiritual tool of posterity. Seeing precedes planning, and then institutionalization.

CHAPTER THREE

LIFE IN THE ANOINTING ORDER

On a daily basis, the life in the Order is concerned with restoration. Nothing is impossible here. It is a life of freedom in a cold cloudy environment, as experienced by Moses in Mount Sinai, Elijah in Mount Horeb and Jesus in Mount Olive. This cloudy environment is the spiritual home of meditation, due to the impregnation of deep thoughts in our hearts. Communication is possible by a defined arrangement and involves visions, dreams, prophecies and teachings. In some cases the voice heard could be loud, while in others it could be a still small voice. In all, the voice is for direction (Isaiah 30:21). Certain thunder strikes could also be avenues for emergency communication as seen in John 12:28-30: ... *Then came there a voice from heaven, saying, I have both glorified it, and will glorify it again. The people therefore, that stood by, and heard it, said that it thundered: others said, an angel spake to him. Jesus answered and said, this voice came not because of me, but for your sakes.* No spiritually conscious person plays with thunder strikes, because it shows the presence of God.

The communication process usually involves: *Ask, and it shall be given you; seek, and ye shall find; knock, and it shall be opened unto you: For every one that asketh receiveth; and he that seeketh findeth; and to him that knocketh it shall be opened.* - Matthew 7:7-8. This shows that the Order expects that we should ask for the Holy Spirit, seek wisdom and enquire from them the secrets of life.

The order of communication could sometimes take after the pattern in 1 Kings 19:11-13: *And he said, Go forth, and stand upon the mount before the Lord. And, behold, the Lord passed by, and a great and strong wind rent the mountains, and brake in pieces the rocks before the Lord; but the Lord was not in the wind: and after the wind an earthquake; but the Lord was not in the earthquake: And after the earthquake a fire; but the Lord was not in the fire: and after the fire a still small voice. And it was so, when Elijah heard it, that he wrapped his face in his mantle, and went out, and stood in the entering in of the cave. And, behold, there came a voice unto him, and said, what doest thou here, Elijah?*

We would see above that Elijah positioned himself by standing upon the mount before the Lord of the Order. Everything is patterned in the Melchizedek Order. A better understanding of this is taking a look at the physical creations we have around us which the Order instituted in place. The

foundation of all that we see physically resides in *El Elyon* –
God most high - who oversees the Melchizedek Order. This
Order is a consciousness order. The reception and
transmission of information are coded in pulsating messages,
similar to the pulse of the heartbeat, and these messages have
to be put together like building blocks before they can make
meanings to those in the physical. Don't forget that our
heartbeat came alive after *El Elyon* breathed into the nostrils
of man. One example would be the languages children use as
they learn how to speak properly. Two children would
understand each other, yet the adult is still trying to figure out
what the child is saying.

The Order boasts of banks of information which have
existed right from the day the world was created till the
present age. It is only the spiritually resilient initiate of the
Order who can get into the archive of knowledge and receive
'Melchizedical' insights and illumination. This attentive
positioning is possible with the kind of eye Jesus referred to
as 'single eye' in Matthew 6:22, and the kind of ear He
expected them to hear with in Matthew 11:15. The purpose
of the anointing is to enable us mature in the things of the
spirit. Jesus questioned Nicodemus' premature knowledge
about the things of the Melchizedek Order when He answered
him: ... *Art thou a master of Israel, and knowest not these things?* -
John 3:10.

The Order communicates mostly in the night, and various instances abide in the Bible as would be seen in 1 Samuel 15:16: *'Stop!' Samuel said to Saul. 'Let me tell you what the Lord said to me last night.'* (NIV).

Whatever is dedicated to God and Anointed belongs to Him, just like the vessels in the Holy Temple in Israel in the days of Solomon. The Angels take charge over items dedicated to God, including your marriage, cars, houses, children, business, etc. This is another reason why denying God your substance of increase, including tithes, is a punishable offence by the Melchizedek Order. You would notice that even the Levites paid a tithe of their tithes. God expects that His servants survive on the tithes that came into the tabernacle, as a means of ensuring the Order would carry out their function.

For example, Abraham had to pay a tithe to Melchizedek, implying that if you will call this Order to protect and bless you, you must also be ready to pay a tithe of all that comes from the Order into your life (Malachi 3:8-10). Failure to do this is seen as robbery by the Order and attracts strong spiritual consequences. The problems the world is experiencing are due to their negligence of the demands of this Order which the Bible sees as the *'Fear of the Lord.'*

We would see a summarized character of the Order from 1 Samuel 15:22,23: *And Samuel said, Hath the Lord as great delight in burnt offerings and sacrifices, as in obeying the voice of the Lord? Behold, to obey is better than sacrifice, and to hearken than the fat of rams. For rebellion is as the sin of witchcraft, and stubbornness is as iniquity and idolatry. Because thou hast rejected the word of the Lord, he hath also rejected thee from being king.*

These verses talk of four things that can move the heart of God – Obedience, Sacrifice, Heeding and Offerings. Out of these four, two are preferred – Obedience and Heeding. That does not mean that the Order does not appreciate sacrifices and offerings in kind. The reason for the two most preferred being Obedience and Heeding is that their negligence disregards God's authority over us, and that is the highest sin any man can commit against the Order, as we can see here - *Then came the word of the Lord unto Samuel, saying, It repenteth me that I have set up Saul to be king: for he is turned back from following me, and hath not performed my commandments* – 1 Samuel 15:10-11.

We would now bring out these four actions of us than can touch the heart of God:

- ■ **Obedience:** Obeying God's command and doing His will is what releases His blessings, making them fall like dew upon the earth. When we disobey Him, we automatically lock up the fountain of heaven and we would be seen suffering. The word of the Lord says: *Go ye therefore, and teach all nations, baptizing them in the name of the Father, and* *of the Son, and of the Holy Ghost: Teaching them to observe all things whatsoever I have commanded you: and, lo, I am with you always, even unto the end of the world. Amen.* (Matthew 28:19-20.) How many of us have actually carried out this commandment?

■ **Sacrifice:** We sacrifice for the work of God either in kind or materially. We have various references to this in the Bible, for instance in Haggai 1:6-11 God says: *Ye have sown much, and bring in little; ye eat, but ye have not enough; ye drink, but ye are not filled with drink; ye clothe you, but there is none warm; and he that earneth wages earneth wages to put it into a bag with holes. Thus saith the Lord of hosts; Consider your ways. Go up to the mountain, and bring wood, and build the house; and I will take pleasure in it, and I will be glorified, saith the Lord. Ye looked for much, and, lo it came to little; and when ye brought it home, I did blow upon it. Why? saith the Lord of hosts. Because of mine house that is waste, and ye run every man unto his own house. Therefore the heaven over you is stayed from dew, and the earth is stayed from her fruit. And I called for a drought upon the land, and upon the mountains, and upon the corn, and upon the new wine, and upon the oil, and upon that which the ground bringeth forth, and upon men, and upon cattle, and upon all the labour of the hands.* These verses prove that God indeed expects us to sacrifice for His work.

■ **Heed:** - To heed means to listen to, observe, regard

instructions and the wisdom to do well and avoid sin. This is the better way, and preferred. To observe is to live the expected life recommended by the Order. A look at 1 Samuel 15 tells us that Saul destroyed the ugly in the war and took the beautiful. This is what we do mostly when we are instructed by God. When the servant of God releases an oracle from the altar, if it pleases us God is the one talking and we would take it with joy, when it offends us the servant is the one talking and we would frown and disobey him. God says in Isaiah 50:10 that obeying God's servant is the quickest way to fearing God, because he hears what God says. Some few weeks ago in the month of August 2012, God said to me: 'I am not wicked, their sins are too much, let them repent. They have rebelled against every instruction I have given in this altar.' And He said further: 'I have raised you as a testimony against them. Now that they have neglected you, they will stretch forth their hands and henceforth will it return with holes.'

- **Offering** – As we have said earlier, offerings are needed to help propagate the gospel of Christ, otherwise the apostles wouldn't have accepted the offerings made in Acts 4:32-37. In the building of the Tabernacle, God advised Moses to receive free will offerings from the Israelites even in their wandering state, to ensure they have the physical arm of the Lord in their midst. Sacrifices and offerings go hand in hand, but sacrifice is more of a soul-binding oath, and it usually costs us more to release than an offering which is free will. Sacrifice is not free will. It is like the widow's mite. A sacrifice moves God to honour your request because you are giving out of scarcity. This is what God did when He gave us Jesus Christ.

Let us see also what the Order expects from the following verses:

1. Genesis 4:7 – Those who do well shall be accepted – **Sacrifice/offering**
2. Isaiah 1:17-18 – Learn to do well, before you can talk with God - **Heeding**
3. Haggai 1:5 – Consider your ways when things are not going well with you rather than blame your predicament upon other people and God - **Obedience**
4. Hosea 4:6-7 – Those who reject the knowledge God are doom to fail in life - **Heeding**

I would encourage you to outline these four actions in your Bible verses as you read and study from today. Also check your daily actions and see if you are on track and are not found wanting by the Order in this regard.

As we have seen above, the Order encourages sacrifices, as offerings, tithes, vows, etc, from those that enjoy its protection and blessings – Psalms 50:5: *Gather to me my* consecrated ones, who made a covenant with me by sacrifice. The sacrifice referred to in Psalms 50:5 was made in 1 Chronicles 29:5-10, when David asked for whoever would support the house of God building project. Such sacrifices are what the Order uses as physical reward for those who officiate at the altar, who they use as their instrument to release information to the physical, and for the building of worship centers, caring for the poor and widows alike as the case may be. Monetary sacrifices are also used in organizing crusades and the printing of evangelical materials. Let us also see how the Bible treats the act of stealing the entitlement that belongs to Order, in Zachariah 5:1-4:

I looked again, and there before me was a flying scroll. 2 He asked me, 'What do you see?' I answered, 'I see a flying scroll, twenty cubits long and ten cubits wide.' 3 And he said to me, 'This is the curse that is going out over the whole land; for according to what it says on one side, every thief will be banished, and according to what it says on the other, everyone who swears falsely will be banished. 4 The Lord Almighty declares, 'I will send it out, and it will enter the house of the thief and the house of anyone who swears falsely by my name. It will remain in that house and destroy it completely, both its timbers and its stones.'

Below are the facts from the verses above:

- The Order issued a decree concerning the punishment pronounced upon anyone who steals. And judging from Malachi 3:8-10, we would say that the Order refers to the act of denying the Order its entitlement.

- The one who steals is also the one who swears falsely, hence both were contained in one scroll.

- The punishment is over the entire land, and by inference all over the world.

- The punishment will live with such persons and ensure he/she does not have peace, as the very foundation of his/her existence will be utterly destroyed.

When provisions are made in the house of God, those who bear the message of the Order and officiate therein can remain in their posts. The practice of allowing the pastors to fend for themselves will only leave them empty, as they may not be able to relate information from the Order as and when needed. Once any of the instruments the Order uses is out of use, the world will suffer for it because they will become easily taken by the devil for lack of knowledge. The information released is for a season, and they are proactive information, aimed at rescuing us from the torture of the devil.

I have seen churches where they place advertisements to employ pastors. While I am not against it, such individuals must have been approved by the Order.

The Order expects that the Anointed, who is their information intermediary, who has a physical existence and life, should be treated with respect and looked after, since the Order's personalities are spiritual and do not live by physical items such as foods, clothing, cars, houses, etc. The provision of these to the Anointed is judged as accepted, as an honour given unto the Order, because the Anointed is the physical arm of the Order on earth who acts as instructed or would otherwise be punished for disobedience, as happened to Moses. If this is the case, the Order expects that physically the Anointed must benefit from the increase in the lives of those who have called on the Order for spiritual protection and blessings: *For God is not unrighteous to forget your work and labour of love, which ye have shewed toward his name, in that ye have ministered to the saints, and do minister.* (Hebrews 6:10).

■ Even our day-to-day communication, either orally or symbolically, is weighed or investigated by the order. Let's see some declarations in respect to this from the Order: *Your words have been stout against me, saith the Lord. Yet ye say, What have we spoken so much against thee? Ye have said, It is vain to serve God: and what profit is it that we have kept his ordinance, and that we have walked mournfully before the Lord of hosts?* And the Bible also says: *But I say unto you, that every idle word that men shall speak, they shall give account thereof in the Day of Judgment.* – Matthew 12:36.

■ The Order appreciates those who do well, who have obeyed the instructions of honour released from the order: *If thou doest well, shalt thou not be accepted? –* Genesis 4:7. This is why Hebrews 11:6 says: *But without faith it is impossible to please him: for he that cometh to God must believe that he is, and that he is a rewarder of them that diligently seek him.* Let us also see what the Order decrees as the reward for obedience to pay tithe, for instance: *... if I will not open you the windows of heaven, and pour you out a blessing, that there shall not be room enough to receive it. And I will rebuke the devourer for your sakes, and he shall not destroy the fruits of your ground; neither shall your vine cast her fruit before the time in the field, saith the Lord of hosts. And all nations shall call you blessed: for ye shall be a delightsome land, saith the Lord of hosts. –* Malachi 3:10-12. Seeing this reward from the Order, it is only a wicked person that will deny the Order his/her tithe, and then would cause the world to experience starvation. When I see people who withhold tithes, I see a wicked soul who is out to ensure the blessings of God ceases from pouring down.

Personalities in the Order
The Order boasts of the following spiritual personalities: the God-head; God the Father, God the Son, and God the Holy Ghost; the Holy angels, souls of departed saints in Abraham's bosom; souls of the prophets of God who died; souls of the

prophets who never saw death but went to heaven; souls of the disciples of Christ; Souls of those connected to Christ who believed in what the disciples preached and those who will be enraptured. This Order will be replicated on earth when the new heaven and new earth come into being.

Order Transformation process

For the Order personalities to appear in a physically visible form there has to be a transformation process. In the days of Jesus, as Moses and Elijah appeared from the Order, the Bible described the process – Luke 9:29-31: *... and went up into a mountain to pray. And as he prayed, the fashion of his countenance was altered, and his raiment was white and glistering. And, behold, there talked with him two men, which were Moses and Elias: Who appeared in glory, and spake of his decease which he should accomplish at Jerusalem.* Here the Order came to release information to the natural, but for the process to take place Jesus had to pray – conditioning Himself to be in the form that could discern their form and hear their voice.

Even as it was time for Him to leave the earth back to the Order, knowing the transformation process it would take, He had to pray and ask if the cup would pass over Him. To enable Him to carry on, an angel from the Order appeared and released a spiritual strength from the Order to strengthen Him – Luke 22:42-44: *Saying, Father, if thou be willing, remove this cup from me: nevertheless not my will, but thine, be done. And there appeared an angel unto him from heaven, strengthening him. And being in an agony he prayed more earnestly: and his sweat was as it were great drops of blood falling down to the ground.* Jesus knows what it takes to invoke the invisible realm of the supernatural – the Melchizedek Order.

While He was about to return into the Order, He forbade Mary not to touch Him until He had ascended back into the Order of immortality, where He would only know joy. Any touch from a human being would have rendered the entire process futile. What does this tell us about our waiting and fasting period? During fasting and prayers we are connecting with the spatial spiritual realm of the Melchizedek Order. If Christ forbade us touching Him, so that He could ascend into the Order, why should anyone even think of having sexual intercourse during a fasting and praying period, as propounded by some pastors?

This is the reason Elijah had to tell Elisha that if he would indeed see him he would receive his heart's desire, because he knew the transformation process that would take place. Upon hearing this information, Elisha had to alert his own spiritual consciousness in order to see, and he saw and confessed. The Order in trying to communicate with mortals would usually try to configure our hearts to begin to feel spiritual pulses. And we would tend to withdraw in passively from the physical in what people usually called absent-mindedness. Then we would start deep thinking. If you take a look at what happened to the prophets of old before God would speak, you will see that the angel would usually asked the servant of God: *what seest thou?* The reason for this question is to confirm if the information has been coded properly into a form that the prophet would be able to discern. Even at this, the ordinary person who has not gained spiritual consciousness will not see anything, as confirmed by Daniel: *And I Daniel alone saw the vision: for the men that were with me saw not the vision; but a great quaking fell upon them, so that they fled to hide…* - Daniel 10:7. So, Daniel had conditioned himself: *In those days I Daniel was mourning three full weeks. I ate no pleasant bread, neither came flesh nor wine in my mouth, neither did I anoint myself at all, till three whole weeks were fulfilled.* – Daniel 10:2-3. This shows that the process of transmitting information from the Order requires that both you and the Order must meet halfway, except in rare cases where the angels have to come in human form, yet it was only Abraham and Lot that knew – the men of Sodom never knew they were angels, for instance.

St. Paul opened our understanding to this fact that an Anointed servant of God hears and speaks both human and spiritual languages, when he said: *Though I speak with the tongues of men and of angels* - 1 Corinthians 13:1. It is this ability that makes the Anointed an intermediary who is used by the Order to disseminate spiritual codes to that on earth and as such the Anointed is seen as one existing in the Earthly Melchizedek Order. We would say therefore that the Anointed is the link between both Orders: Heavenly Melchizedek and Earthly Melchizedek Order.

We saw that in Exodus 20:18-19 the entire earth experienced a shock as God was about to make an appearance to the children of Israel, yet they only saw His back: *And all the people saw the thunderings, and the lightnings, and the noise of the trumpet, and the mountain smoking: and when the people saw it, they removed, and stood afar off. And they said unto Moses, Speak thou with us, and we will hear: but let not God speak with us, lest we die.*

Some people had wondered why these experiences are not commonplace today. In fact they are still very common. It is only that we have become dead spiritually, and are not ready to invoke His presence.

The Burning Bush event, which brought the angel that spoke with Moses, is another example. This transformation process is what explains the power in the Order. Miracles happen when the Order does a spiritual repair or full human parts replacement, as the Order did by converting the rib of Adam into a full human being. This is why the Order would want to take something from you, bless it, make it into an entity that you would appreciate and institute it to be.

Appearance from the Order into the natural

The personalities in the Order create a sense of vision in whoever they want to appear to:

- God appeared to Adam and Eve in the cool of the evening. First he was not there, then Adam heard His footstep.

- God also appeared when He smelled the sweet savour of Abel's sacrifice and His appearance was referred to as His presence. This is why He told Cain that if he did well, he would be accepted by the Order. The Order appreciates acts of dedication and sacrifice.

- He appeared to Abraham in a voice.

- He appeared to Noah in a voice.

- He wrestled with Jacob as a man.

- The Lord appeared to Abraham again, this time as men who were going to destroy Sodom and Gomorrah.

- The Angel appeared to Daniel and Daniel confirmed that he alone saw the angel.

- Moses and Elijah appeared to Jesus in the transfiguration, because they live their afterlife in a sub-order of the Order because of their righteousness before God. An example of such sub-order is called the 'Abraham's Bosom,' a place of comfort after the death of the righteous- Luke 16:22-23. Other sub-orders are the Levitical Order, the Salvation Order, The Sainthood Order, The Priesthood Order, The Prophethood Order, The Flaming Fire Order, and so on.

■ The Angels appeared to the women who went to the grave site of Jesus.

■ Jesus appeared to two young men in a form different from that by which they knew Him – Mark 16:12.

All these appearances points to the fact that the spiritual Melchizedek Order is as real as we would behold our own face in the mirror; it only depends how we dedicate our time to search for the hidden wisdom that leads to light – Jesus, the Power and Wisdom of God.

Disappearance from the natural into the Order

The easiest way for these personalities to leave the physical realm into the Order is by a process called 'vanishing' (Luke 24:31), which the Bible sometime calls 'disappearing'. This is why St Paul says that those who are of this Order cannot be examined by physical standard, because they are above earthly human understanding (1 Corinthians 2:14-15).

In all these we see that the Order's presence only came into being in what the Bible termed appearances. We would also see that they can appear only to whoever they want to appear to in the form they like – as thunderous voices and as a wind – Acts 2, as a cloud – Psalm 104:4, or as human – Genesis 17&18. To tell of the power of the Order, we would see how Nebuchadnezzar was turned into an animal which had to live among animals in the forest, eating and living with them. The

Order can provide and depose anyone of his/her earthly treasures. The most valued possession in the Order is 'Power,' hence Jesus says that all power has been given unto Him.

The Place of Blood in the Order

Scripture tells us that the Order overcame the devil by the blood of the Lamb. This is a top spiritual secret which resides in the secret place of the Almighty (Psalms 91:1). Only the spiritually minded can assimilate this. Why blood in the first place? The Order values blood because for the earth to exist the Lamb was slain from the foundation of the earth: ... *the book of life of the Lamb slain from the foundation of the world.* (Revelations 13:8). The Order has instituted a process of admission into the book of life of the Lamb, which is why we are in this discussion. Whosoever is admitted experiences and lives a life of the Anointing Order. In the spiritual realm, there is no need for blood. The purpose of blood is to give life to our mortal body. The blood decays in nature. As we grow old, the blood withers out until we have little at old age because the bone marrow stops manufacturing it. Why? The human body decays on a daily basis because of the presence of decaying substances in the body which reside in the earth and form part of the human body – the blood for instance is made of iron. The bone contains calcium. Our urine contains ammonia, and so on.

Why did Jesus resurrect with His body? We would see that the body of Moses was contended by the devil. The devil, prior to his fall, belonged to the Melchizedek Order, where only truth and good prevail. There is no knowledge of evil there, because what causes deadness to the soul is evil. When the devil left the Order, he formed his own Order – the Melchiresha order.

Though this order of the devil is spiritual, it survives with blood because he cannot ascend and remain in the abode of God which does not survive on blood. This was why God was angry with Cain over the blood of Abel which cried to Him in heaven. All devilish meetings are fed with evil knowledge from this Melchiresha order. The only way any one from the spiritual Order can live on earth is to have blood – hence Jesus had to shed His blood in our place, as the devil would stop at nothing to ensure he takes human bloods to remain on earth after his banishment from Heaven, so that whenever we partake in the communion, the Order transforms the wine into the blood of the Lamb that was actually sacrificed from the foundation of the earth (Revelation 13:8), and as long as that blood lives inside of us, the devil will avoid us.

At the same time the Order transforms the bread into the body of Christ – a resilient and willing nature of the Order. From the days of Abel, man had sacrificed burnt offerings to God until our Lord Jesus came to institute a new order as required by the Melchizedek Order, because the devil had started receiving blood and human sacrifices from idolaters through his idols. The Order causes the earth to experience dynamic evolution at all times through decrees, as happened in the beginning. Knowing that the devil was imprisoning more souls in chains daily through idolatry, Jesus volunteered to come to earth to institute the Earthly Melchizedek Order (EMO), where all those who do the will of God can share fellowship together in one accord and receive spiritual information from the Order to refine the world. The Melchizedek Order, the Heavenly Melchizedek Order (HMO) and the Earthly Melchizedek Order (EMO), operate in a transmitter-receiver mode. Christ's preaching revealed this when He said: '*the Kingdom of God is at hand*', and it became possible after Christ instituted the Holy Communion. This was the original intention of God for keeping Adam in that Garden of Eden because He was creating an extension of His kingdom which would be physical, and would enable man to relate with Him as the angels do in Heaven. The earth is His footstool, and His intention is to walk as He feels through the earth in a form that the human sense would discern.

To understand this better we have to see scriptural evidence of how God visited the earth on various occasions through His signs and wonders – the pillars of clouds and of fire, the voice that spoke to Samuel, and many other instances. A study of the creation events would tell us that God is always in the business of investigating and assessing what exists on earth, which had responded to the decree from the Order. This act is what the Bible represented in Genesis 1 &2 as: 'and God saw that it was good'.

The Earthly Order's duty is to create the atmosphere for the Heavenly Order to bring to pass requests made through prayers by the faithful servants of God. While man was in that garden, God carried out a trial assessment of the functionality of man and how he would eventually respond to him when He brought the animals for him to name. Everything went as planned and His heart was glad, until the fateful day when he saw that Adam could not relate with the Order to get the kind of wisdom that would help him achieve much. Adam was struggling with so many things and God decided to get him help. This help was actually the wisdom residing in the Order.

This is where the woman comes into creation – to be that element through which the Order could eventually persuade the man to act as the Order expects. This would be seen over time as women easily get away with most of the demands they put forward to men. If the devil had not fused the woman, and also deceived her, the earth would have been perfect with her creation. It was this failure that brought about the sacrifice of our Lord Jesus, whose blood paid for all our atrocities. Have you wondered why some ladies are christened, 'Angel' during their naming? We know who angels are and what they do.

The Creation of Woman by the Order

There are two things the Bible says have prices greater than rubies: wisdom (Job 28:18) and the virtuous woman (Proverbs 31:10), meaning that the virtuous woman is an embodiment of wisdom. When God came down to see Adam, it was the intention of God that Adam received a help that would link him to the Order, so that even while God was not there to share fellowship with him, the help would be there to represent the care of the Order. The woman was created as one who could be easily used by the Order so that she could function as one speaking from the Order, similar to a computer which operates on whichever operating system is installed. The hardware is unchangeable, but the computer's operation can be manipulated through software. To accomplish this, the Order requested the rib of the man as a raw material so that he would respond to the woman's ideas and appreciate her presence in his life, which is why Ecclesiastes 9:9 says that the woman is man's only reward here on earth. The woman was created with a mind of the Order in her, which would make her respond to the commands Order, in order to fulfill her obligation as the help to her husband, in wisdom and understanding. Today we see that every successful man boasts of a woman behind him who dumps wisdom in the form of pulsating codes in his heart, which he would regurgitate later, turning them into action statements and putting them to work.

Naturally, the woman is created with more spiritual sensitivity than the man. Why? God took a rib from man and transformed it into a creature which He presented to man, and Adam's joy shows that the woman was as perfect as the God who brought her to him and thereafter, the woman, we were told, discussed with the serpent, and would later persuade her husband to accept the fruit of the tree. What does this tell us? The woman can easily detect a spiritual scene and would get ready to react if she had not done so. I know some would argue this. This is my candid opinion about the woman and this fact can be buttressed with stories in the Bible of women who walked with God. Mary the mother of Jesus is one of such women representing the purpose of woman on earth.

The woman was created to be jealous, emotional, possessive, caring, defensive, creative, decisive, corrective, firm and mindful of her environment. It is still easy to see these attributes in women, though many apply them with devil's intent, which is actually what the devil achieved by possessing her at the garden. Adam didn't know all these attributes of her, but the devil knew, I suppose. So the devil, who had left the Order quickly, went and possessed her in order to manipulate whatever he wanted to show or speak to her husband.

When Adam saw his wife in physical form, the devil was already inside her. The book of Ezekiel 28:13 says: *Thou hast been in Eden the garden of God; every precious stone was thy covering, the sardius, topaz, and the diamond, the beryl, the onyx, and the jasper, the sapphire, the emerald, and the carbuncle, and gold: the workmanship of thy tabrets and of thy pipes was prepared in thee in the day that thou wast created.* The devil is handsome, attractive and a musician. This attraction was what deceived Eve and she fell for the devil's tricks. This is also the reason why today many women still love fanciful and precious stone jewellery. Women also love those who sing and play musical instruments.

This is what the Order wanted to use the woman for, to feed her with wisdom any time they wanted to talk to the man and make him carry out actions that the Order required of him. This would make it easy for him to achieve much without waiting for God to come into the garden to tell him what to do. As usual on other days, God came into that Garden to assess progress made by man in the application of his wisdom now that the woman was with him, only to find that the man and his wife had fallen from his Order and as such now wore a nature that appreciated evil. Since man was already aware of evil, his mind would become corrupt and live a life of suspicion which would further degenerate into hatred. God knew that leaving them in the garden would make them eat the fruit of the tree of life, which would make them live in the appreciation of evil forever, just like the devil.

The plan the devil was hatching was to mutilate the seed of the woman as she brought forth, because until then Adam hadn't known his wife sexually, which would have made her bear a seed that would favour the righteous course of the Order. If the devil had not possessed the woman, her womb would have borne only righteous seeds. The Order gave the woman the womb to enable God to form children there as He confirmed in Jeremiah 1:4-5: *Then the word of the Lord came unto me, saying, Before I formed thee in the belly I knew thee; and before thou camest forth out of the womb I sanctified thee, and I ordained thee a prophet unto the nations.*

What God would have had on earth would have been the replication of the Order's values, as the children were being possessed by the thought and wish of the Order. So the devil, being aware of what the Order had done, and knowing that Adam was ignorant of the plan of the Order, quickly came to mutilate the body of the woman so as to possess whatever seed she brought forth thereafter. The woman sold her soul to the devil the moment she fell for his antics, and would over time be under the influence of the devil. From the curse God placed on the serpent in Genesis 3:15: *And I will put enmity between thee and the woman...*, we would see the level of possession of the woman by evil forces all over the world until they are born-again in Christ. The latter part of that curse says: *between thy seed and her seed; it shall bruise thy head, and thou shalt bruise his heel.* So we would see that every child born into this world, except those Anointed from the womb by God as holy vessels unto Him, will have the devil's wisdom to contend with. This may be the reason why many children carry out evil ideas without being taught, because this seems to be the default character inherent in them.

The devil causes an internal revolt in most women who don't have the heart of God in them by sowing a seed of discontent and then suspicion in them, so that they quarrel over little things as they disagree. He turns the woman's heart to appreciating fanciful material things, and her duty as one who would have been able to receive wisdom from the Order is lost to the deception of the devil. With this in place, man would suffer on earth as he tries to do things without wisdom. So to save this situation, the Order thought it wise to raise men and women who would become their physical information bearers on earth, through the process we now call anointing. In the old days, before Jesus came, this process was unable to admit so many people at the same time into this Earthly Melchizedek Order which they were trying to institute.

David got wind of it when he was able to describe the presence of God as would be seen in Psalm 104:1-4, for instance: *Bless the Lord, O my soul. O Lord my God, thou art very great; thou art clothed with honour and majesty. Who coverest thyself with light as with a garment: who stretchest out the heavens like a curtain: Who layeth the beams of his chambers in the waters: who maketh the clouds his chariot: who walketh upon the wings of the wind: Who maketh his angels spirits; his ministers a flaming fire:* This is what attracted David to plead with God to allow him build Him a temple so that the EMO would be instituted in his time. This has been achieved by Jesus through the institution of the Holy Communion and the pouring of God's spirit upon the earth. Never in the history of the world has there been the abundance of God's wisdom and power commonplace on earth as it is since that day. And now Jesus is saying to us daily: *anyone that is tasty should come and drink from the fountain of living waters.* Meaning that it is our personal decision and effort that can take us into the path of light.

The Power in the Order
The Order boasts of enormous powers, such as can melt mountains. It is the power we must rely on to get out of our predicaments. The Bible says in Isaiah 31:1: *Woe to them that go down to Egypt for help and stay on horses, and trust in chariots, because they are many; and in horsemen, because they are very*

strong; but they look not unto the Holy One of Israel, neither seek the Lord!

There is enormous power that is self sustaining, so why look elsewhere? I am inviting you to get initiated into the Order, where you will have no regrets in life any more. I have been enjoying it since I got initiated. Miracles are possible when this power is activated. A sick person can only become healed when the Order is present. This is why it is a requirement to create the environment that will attract the Order, as Jesus did in His transfiguration. While I am not against the present day over-popularized praise and worship sessions in churches, which in most cases is not accepted by God, the congregation need to physically experience the presence of the Order before they can worship and praise God in truth and in spirit because it is the *spirit that quickeneth*, meaning that the spirit must have taken possession of the hearts, minds and souls of the congregation there present.

Sub-Orders of the Anointing Order
It is important at this juncture for us to explain some of the sub-orders that exist within the Anointing Order. These include the Levitical Order, the Salvation Order, The Sainthood Order, The Royal Priesthood Order, The Prophethood Order, The Flaming Fire Order, and so on. We would now discuss them in turn:

The Levitical Priesthood Order:

This order is a replica of the service of angels who minister before the throne of God, here on earth to provide a sort of a reflection of what goes on before the throne of God. In the Old Testament tabernacle, the mercy seat is likened to the seat of the Father where the golden altar resides. The Levitical priests officiated in burning incense before the Lord. They minister in songs unto God. These service would be placed side by side with what the angels do in heaven in Revelation 14:2-5 and Revelations 8:3.

The Salvation Order:

The Salvation Order came into being after the death of Jesus Christ at the Cross for the remission of our sins. Prior to the institution of this Sub- Order of the Melchizedek Order, the prophets did yearn for it but they only saw the shadow of it coming years ahead of them – 1 Peter 1:9-12: *Receiving the end of your faith, even the salvation of your souls. Of which salvation the prophets have enquired and searched diligently, who prophesied of the grace that should come unto you: ... Unto whom it was revealed, that not unto themselves, but unto us ....* Even Abraham, in all his righteous acts before God, only saw the days of the Salvation Order. Because he was aware of what the Order would bring to mankind, he indeed rejoiced – John 8:56: *'Your father Abraham rejoiced to see My day, and he saw it and was glad.* Someone may be a prophet, a pastor and a healing minister and do all manner of works in the vineyard, yet not be saved and preserved in the Salvation Order. Salvation could be lost when we are out of the Order's circle of influence. It is like what would happen to water creatures taken out of water and kept of land. Over time, that creature would die. The only way we can make heaven is when we are in registered in this Order. This is the Order where all restored souls belong. Anyone who is initiated into it and stays until implanted does everything with the fear of the Lord. Many have asked why some indeed do preach the gospel yet still live in sin, the truth is that they have no salvation yet. Remember that in John 4:23 Jesus says that salvation belongs to some people - those who have God living in their heart, who then worship God in spirit and in truth. This is the Order of the fifth seal revealed in Revelation 6:9-11: *And when he had opened the fifth seal, I saw under the altar the souls of them that were slain for the word of God, and for the testimony which they held: And they cried with a loud voice, saying, How long, O Lord, holy and true, dost thou not judge and avenge our blood on them that dwell on the earth? And white robes were given unto every one of them; and it was said unto them, that they should rest yet for a little season, until their fellow servants also and their brethren, that should be killed as they were, should be fulfilled.* This is the Order of long suffering (Revelation 7:10), which we would be able to endure when we have the 'Christine' consciousness.

The Sainthood Order:

This Order registers the names of those who are willing to readily sacrifice unto the work of the Lord, an activity which keeps them consecrated before the Lord. A verse of the Bible that revealed this Order is Psalms 50:5: *Gather my saints together unto me; those that have made a covenant with me by sacrifice.* God values that hard work and sacrifice towards the course of His kingdom on earth and as such protects them from the affliction of the devil so that they would be harvested one by one and preserved for redemption. This is because the Lord rewards those who diligently seek Him – Hebrews 11:6. In the book of Revelation 7:3 we would see that God is in search of His saints, who also are part of His servants and would eventually mark them to be saved: *Saying, Hurt not the earth, neither the sea, nor the trees, till we have sealed the servants of our God in their foreheads.* So every good work you are doing for the sake of the gospel, it is not an effort in futility, go ahead with the good work, He is El Roi – He sees and would reward every faithful servant at the end of the day. In Revelation 16:4-6, John distinguishes between 'saints' and 'prophets'. Why? Because these are all sub-orders of the Melchizedek Order.

The Royal Priesthood Order:

This was revealed in Paul's writing in 1 Peter 2:9-10: *But ye are a chosen generation, a royal priesthood, an holy nation, a peculiar people; that ye should shew forth the praises of him who hath called you out of darkness into his marvellous light; Which in time past were not a people, but are now the people of God: which had not obtained mercy, but now have obtained mercy.* Take note of the last line - *but now have obtained mercy.* It is only when we are initiated into this Order in our thoughts and actions that we may obtain the mercies of the Lord, which is the reason why He will send His angels and Holy Spirit to be around you. What is the difference between this Order and the Levitical Priesthood Order? The Royal Order allows one to communicate with God directly because we now have the mind of God through Jesus Christ, who had revealed Him to us, and through the Holy Spirit, who teaches us what we need to do to merit the favour of God daily. The Levitical Order depended on Moses to hear from God. Those in the Royal Priesthood Order hear God directly. One morning I heard a voice say to me: 'you have been called into a Royal Priesthood Order.' My spiritual alertness has improved since then. Wherever I turn I hear what the spirit says. This makes it possible to read the thoughts of hearts, as Jesus did severally when He had to tell the disciples what thought they harboured in their hearts.

The Prophethood Order: This Order is where all those who will reveal the heart of God prophetically exists. The Prophethood Order is like a school of training, similar to those in the Old Testament often referred to as school of the prophets.

Flaming Fire Order: In Psalms 104:4 this Order was briefly revealed. This is the Order in which all ministers of the Lord are initiated. They speak with thunderous voices, challenging everyone to put away evil and seek repentance. All preachers of the gospel who are willing to go against the crowd to bring to pass the word of the Lord are registered, and functions in this sub-Order. This is the Elijah and King David's Order. Moses also was in this Order hence he was so zealous for the work of God.

The Musical Order: Sound involves the vibration of an air column. Science has found that every sound we make has a sinusoidal wave with wavelength, frequency, amplitude and a wave band. Human and instrument sounds have also been classified into soprano, alto, tenor, baritone and bass. We also have low, mid and high frequencies. A look at musical instruments will show how humans have been able to commune with the spiritual realm to represent the sounds they hear in their subconscious state in the physical. Music is possible when an unseen voice speaks in our mind and then energizes our conscious state to respond to the song. Music is the quickest way to get possessed by spirits. This is because it contains rhythmic cyclical sonar vibrations. The cyclical nature of the beats helps it to activate the human spirit. Funnily enough, these beats synchronize with our heartbeats. Music initiates us on a daily basis into either the Order of God or that of the devil. The devil was the chief musician in heaven and he created his own music order here on earth, where he initiates worldly musicians. The devil's music order is filled with violence and self praise, the devil's characteristics. This causes the destruction of the souls of those initiated into the devil's order. The music of the Order of God can be seen from Revelation 14:2-4. Music is the easiest way to gather the hosts of heaven together, which is why the Bible says that God dwells in the midst of His praise (Psalm 22:3). When we praise God in music, He yearns to save our soul from destruction - 2 Chronicles 20:22: *As they began to sing and praise, the Lord set ambushes against the men of Ammon and Moab and Mount Seir who were invading Judah, and they were defeated* (NIV). You will notice when you sing and pray intermittently, your prayers are ordered, purer and focused because of the ordered nature of music. You will see yourself replicating the music cycle in your prayers also – Ephesians 5:19: *speaking to one another with psalms, hymns, and songs from the Spirit. Sing and make music from your heart to the*

Lord (NIV). Notice that the verse says Christians should communicate in music. There is no Sunday the Lord would not give me a new song to sing before the sermon. And the song would reveal the heart of God to the congregation. This enables the message to flow spiritually. Music sets the pace for spiritual communication.

The book of Psalms in the Bible explains this better. Music attracts the spirits, and when we hear music and become transformed we begin to hear what the spirit says. This is a powerful instrument of prophecy. We have full initiates, those who live in and by music, and we also have intermittent initiates, those who don't have the gift to play musical instruments and also compose songs, they rather consume what the full initiate produces. Those who live in the Order are seen almost every day composing songs and using their mouths to play the supposed accompaniment instruments as heard from the Order. We would see that any time the evil spirit tormented Saul, the anointed sounds of the harp from David draw him out of the devil's torment into the music of the Order of God, and Saul would become calm. When we sing before the Lord, we often take oaths unknowingly because it is done on our behalf by our human spirit. All the vows I have made before the Lord happen when I am in the music realm. Music can make you yield your strength to another or it can make you defensive. Most women and men fell in love when they heard music that took away their unwillingness. Before they knew it, they were in each other's arms.

Violent music makes one violent and defensive, as seen in violent rap, hip pop and R&B music. This is why many take drugs to experience the devil's world all the time, because they seem not to be comfortable with the orderliness created by man in the real world.

Music can give you a bold spirit or a frail one. It all depends on the instruments played, the beat pattern, the voice of the singer and the dance steps. Anyone who wants to hear what the angels are saying should consider getting initiated into the Music Order of God by learning how to play a musical instrument, especially the electronic keyboard or piano. You can even learn music production in the studio. You won't regret the experience.

These Orders explained above have also prompted many to set up various associations for the purpose of upholding the objectives of the gospel, but they have also been bastardized by political greed in their midst, thereby rendering the purpose of the institution meaningless. I believe this explains what the Melchizedek Order and the various sub-Orders stand to achieve; to foster unity, wholesomeness of purpose and dedication to the restoration plan of God.

My initiation and admission into the Order

St Paul says that God considered him worthy and then called him into ministry - 1 Timothy 1:12: *I thank Christ Jesus our Lord, who has given me strength, that he considered me trustworthy, appointing me to his service* (NIV). After the Lord called me and the church had commenced, I needed to start functioning in line with the dictates of the Order, and to be initiated into the Order of illuminative teaching. Just as it happened to Samuel, who was to become a prophet, and God had to test his ability to hear spiritual voice. It was at 5.30 am on the 14th of December 2008 when I saw myself in the learning environment, more like in the wilderness, with many tents. Each of these tents had a teacher disseminating the heart of God to his students. I came into the tent that was close to the entrance of the camp, and my teacher instructed me to get a notebook to write down whatever he said. That was how I got the spirit that has empowered me to write and teach.

Ever since that morning I can hardly explain the way it has been. The Order just gets me to do what God wants. The strength comes whenever it is time to work for the Order and my mouth will be filled with songs of vows to render my heart or adoration before God. Many of us have also been given the opportunity to become admitted into the Order, but our lack of understanding has made it difficult to receive it. If you have ever seen your pastor in a dream teaching you, then you are on your way to becoming admitted. If you can compose songs of worship from your inner voice, and play a musical instrument in a pattern determined by a voice speaking inside you, you are on your way into the Order. What you should be discovering now is who your pastor is, because you will receive whatever spirit is in him as he continuously teaches you. Caution! Listening to someone will always infuse you with the spirit in him or her.

CHAPTER FOUR

SECRETS IN THE ANOINTING ORDER

The Anointing Order is the home of top secrets. These secrets can only be revealed through the Anointed who has been admitted into the learning Order as seen in Ezekiel 1:3: *The word of the Lord came to Ezekiel the priest...*(NIV). Ezekiel was a priest, an Anointed servant of God, hence he could hear God speak. This is found in several parts of the Bible.

Here the Lord teaches the Anointed what he/she needed to know so that he/she can release others from their burden. Scripture says: *Surely you desire truth in the inner parts; you teach me wisdom in the inmost place.* – Psalms 51:6 (NIV). The 'inmost place' mentioned in the scripture we just read is the secret place of the most high God – the Melchizedek Anointing Order. As the Anointed tries to find rest for his/her soul, he/she meets with the Lord of the Order through His angels, in prayers, and these secrets are released. This implies that, where there is no asking, there is no revelation. It was only Daniel who could reveal the handwriting on the wall. These are the codes I am talking about. Top secrets from the

Order are often framed in messages which are revealed in dreams and visions. Only the Anointed can interpret what they see and extract meanings from them to help solve problems on earth.

On 20th March 2009, the Lord gave me a revelation of things to come and I sent it out as an email to some people then: 'There is going to be nine years of economic recession starting from this year 2009. There will be mass unemployment and hunger everywhere, but God will favour His children during this period. They will have enough to eat and even give out. The world will turn to believers for rescue - to be fed and provided for. Those who engage in ungodly business pursuits will be hit hard. Those who have not stored for God will lose everything they had laboured for. People will be in debt and many banks will close down. The world will experience real crises - not war but complaints and dissatisfaction everywhere. GOD is doing this so that the world will turn to him.

What to do during this period:
1. Repent from every form of false life.
2. Do the will of God - win souls into God's kingdom.
4. Be found worthy of God always.
5. Live a blameless life.
6. God is going to favour you so that you can provide for His children.

Even as I write this book, the Lord keeps reminding me of this revelation. We can read through and understand Psalm 15 to get used to the qualities of who God is expecting to be in His tabernacle.

The Anointing Order does not throw information anyhow, as the devil does. For Moses to get the Ten Commandments he had to stay for 40 days and nights on the cold top of mount Horeb. To hear from God, Elijah had to run to mount Horeb. But, even, then, there is always an easy way out. This is what the Anointed searches for – the easy way out. In the Old Testament people spend days fasting and praying without an answer, but Jesus wants us to obey His command and win souls to experience success in life. Moses was on top of the mountain fasting and seeking the face of God and before he came down the people had gone astray. If you must put on sackcloth to fast and pray and avoid the work of evangelism, then you are working the hard way. Jesus says that when we fast we should anoint our heads and appear decent in public as a means to aiding the works of evangelism. While you are hiding and praying, ask yourself what is happening to the souls in the street. The Anointed think of what Christ would have done if He was still on earth. Daniel spent days fasting and praying, confessing his sins and those of his ancestors: *While I was speaking and praying, confessing my sin and the sin of my people Israel and making my request to the Lord my God for his holy hill* (Daniel 9:20 NIV). It was the sins referred to here that made the Prince of Persia delay the angel from coming to give him answer (Daniel 10:12-13). If we don't own the devil he won't have anything against him. Following Jesus is the easy way out. So the Anointed seeks to know the secrets that will make life more bearable for him.

Some of the top secrets that are available to us today from the Bible were the efforts of some people like us who decided to invoke the presence of God, and not let things be the way they were. They were moved with pity to ask the creator of the universe why things where as they were.

Some have said that some of the revealed secrets now contained in the Bible are no longer useful in our generation. This is a fallacy. The Order is the same yesterday, today and forever. This is seen in St. Paul's description of Melchizedek. Every revealed secret is to ensure we are able to learn the ways of the Order so that we may be protected and blessed by it. This is why Jesus says that His words and actions were only a fulfilment of what the Order has instituted and still expects.

In the section that follows, we see these top secrets revealed, and what effort led to their release, so that we could also learn to pursue the same process and find rest upon our souls, because the more we have peace, the longer we may live on earth to do the will of God.

1. Noah's Ark: Noah heard from God and he built an ark to save his family. He was righteous even when everyone had gone astray.
2. The Tabernacle: Moses heard God because he was humble and God revealed the tabernacle to him. It was first of its kind and God dwelt in their midst.
3. Nebuchadnezzar's Dream interpretation: Daniel went to pray and seek the face of God, and the secret was revealed to him. Nebuchadnezzar had the dream because he was thinking of what would happen in the future.
4. The Lord's Prayer: The disciples were with Jesus and then they watched Him and then asked Him to teach them how to pray.
5. 'Born Again, Born of Water and Spirit': Nicodemus saw the need to change his way of life as he saw Jesus daily displaying the power of God in their midst.
6. The Power of Fasting and Prayer: The disciples tried to heal an epilepsy patient but were not successful. They watched Jesus do it with ease and then they asked to know why they had not been successful.

Now, in my deepest enquiry about the reason why Men of God were renowned people in the Bible and even in our present dispensation, why they have so much regard, possess so much power and authority that even leaders at the helms of power accord them such respects, and why many are successful in their careers apart from their pastoral jobs, I am led into the truths I now write in this book. It was my desire to ensure that everyone should have access to this wisdom in a practical way to enable them to understand what the presence of the anointing could do in their chosen career, making them more productive in whatever they did. The secrets have been written in my books, starting from my first, 'Existing in the Supernatural,' to this tenth book, 'Gifted and Anointed,' and more secrets are yet to be released. Today I can see the difference in my life. For three years and nine months since God started me on this journey on the new path I am not used to, I have seen increased wisdom, which is renewed every morning, to better my life. There is no ending to the knowledge the Order reveals to those who subscribe to it.

Some Laws of the Melchizedek Order

1. No asking. No receiving. No seeking. No finding. (Matthew 7:7).

2. Asking must be done in line with a specified manner; you don't ask because you feel like asking. Whatever you demand to be fulfilled by the Order must be in line with the character of the Order – see Philippians 4:8.

3. To whom much is given, much is demanded – Luke 12:48.

4. Every vow made or oath taken before the Order must be redeemed – Ecclesiastes 5: 1-2.

5. Love your neighbours as you love yourself and do not hate your enemies (Matthew 5:44).

6. Settle every quarrel you have with anybody before coming into the presence of the Order (Matthew 5:23-24).

7. Let no fellow brethren lay a complaint of sin against you. Every complaint of sin will be investigated and judged accordingly. If found guilty in sin, then your prayers will be an abomination before the Order – Genesis 18:20-21.

8. You must release wealth materially to care for the welfare of the Anointed, who is the earthly representative of the Order – Jesus had Judas as His treasurer, He values the widow's mite and also told the disciples to abide in whichever home accepted them and should eat there – Mark 12:41-44, Luke 10:4-8.

9. The Dead shall be judged and the guilty shall be sentenced to eternal condemnation in hell – Revelation 20:12.

10. The Order hates divorce and any brethren who hates his spouse will not be heard when he prays – Malachi 2:16.

11. No wife should do her husband evil all the days of her life.

12. You must obey every instruction from the Order. Obedience is better than sacrifice – 1 Samuel 15:22.

13. Those who kill by the sword will likewise die by the sword – Matthew 26:52.

14. Once a thief is caught he/she would remit what he/she had stolen seven times over – Proverbs 6:31.

15. Your service to God must be wholehearted. No one, having put his/her hand on the plough, should look back. Idleness is not tolerated – Luke 9:62.

16. You must keep on praying for labourers to carry out the will of the Order. Do not slumber; else the enemy will sow his seeds among you – Matthew 9:38.

17. You must keep the love and fellowship of brethren through the Holy Communion. It is mandatory to be present in all brotherhood meetings and functions – Hebrews 10:25.

18. No discrimination among brethren – no male or female, neither tribal difference. Everyone is equal before the Order – Galatians 3:28.

19. Any talent not employed will be taken away and given to those who would make profitable use of it – Matthew 13:12.

20. Every word that comes out of our mouths shall be weighed and judged – Matthew 12:36.

Blasphemy is a punishable offence and will never be forgiven. It is the easiest way to be condemned in hell. Mocking those used by the Order as instruments of communication is seen as mocking the Holy Spirit of the Order – Mark 3:29.

Facts about Secrets from the Order

1. The release of secrets from the Order is done for the purpose of making us able to do the will of God and in saving lives from the pit of destruction – Deuteronomy 29:29, 1 Corinthians 2:7-8.

2. The hearer of the secret must reveal the secret exactly as the Order wants it – John 12:49.

3. The revealed secrets are often hidden in physical sacraments – John 13:5-8.

4. Miracles are the physical manifestation of the secrets from the Order – John 10:25.

5. The secret unites everyone back to the Order so that they would hear the voice of the Lord of the Order – John 10:14-16.

6. Keeping and doing the terms of the revealed secrets is seen as a show of love for the Order – John 14:15.

7. Anyone who bears the secret is protected from the enemy

to enable the secret to be taught to those who need it to better their lives – John 14:18.

8. Only those who have the Christ consciousness are qualified to ask for anything from the Order – John 15:4 -7.

9. The secrets are made know when anyone from the Order teaches the seeker – John 15:15.

10. The Order releases secrets to those do not go astray from God – John 16:1.

11. Secrets are released to those who would remember them and use them when needed – John 15:20.

12. Secrets are released to those who persistently ask – John 16:18.

13. The secret bearer is the Spirit of Truth – John 16:13.

CHAPTER FIVE

THE EXPLOITS OF THE ANOINTED

There is a verse in the Bible that spells out good works: Isaiah 60:1: *Arise, shine; for thy light is come, and the glory of the Lord is risen upon thee.* The 'glory of the Lord' is the Anointing from the Order. 'Touch not my Anointed' is what the Bible says, showing that there is someone God calls His Anointed. The existence of top spiritual secrets which culminate in wisdom needed to make this world a better place is the reason behind the Lord looking for those He would anoint into the Order so that there would be here on earth, the diffused presence of God. These are people God created with a special task ahead of them which they would carry out to deliver the children of God from the grip of sin. Sin wipes all the good things God intends to do in your life out of your path. The spirit of the God can make anyone to do what we wouldn't have been able to do as seen in Haggai 1:14: *And the Lord stirred up the spirit of Zerubbabel the son of Shealtiel, governor of Judah, and the spirit of Joshua the son of Josedech, the high priest, and the spirit of all the remnant of the people; and they came and did work in the house of the Lord of hosts, their God.* How did this happen? – it was due to the word of the Lord spoken through His prophet (Haggai 1:1).

The Order is looking for recruits who will become intermediaries to convey information to the physical. But for this to happen, the Order expects that the elects and the people who are in pain must make a request to the Lord of the Order through prayers which would be reviewed by the Order: *When he saw the crowds, he had compassion on them, because they were harassed and helpless, like sheep without a shepherd. Then he said to his disciples, 'The harvest is plentiful but the workers are few. Ask the Lord of the harvest, therefore, to send out workers into his harvest field.'* – Matthew 9:36-38 (NIV).

This is to fulfill the main task of the Order, which is to harvest the sons and daughters of God back to Him in an eternal project called 'RESTORATION' – Isaiah 42:22: *But this is a people robbed and spoiled; they are all of them snared in holes, and they are hid in prison houses: they are for a prey, and none delivereth; for a spoil, and none saith, Restore.*

Then a call is made which many will respond to but due to the intricate nature of the job of restoration, few will finally yield their hearts, and they will become those who are chosen, which will then be Anointed: *For many are called, but few are chosen.* – Matthew 22:14. These recruits are then trained and spiritually empowered to execute the will of the Order here on earth – by which all men shall come to know Him, the I am that I am, El Elyon, as God. From this premise, we now know who the Anointed is and his/her duty call.

I use the word 'exploits' to refer to a notable achievement, feat, deed, effort, great work, etc. We are made to know in 1 Corinthians 1:24 that the Anointed is one filled with power and wisdom of God. Many of us are good at seeking the wisdom of God, but we hardly put it to work and then we would lose the power of God. Exploits come when the power and wisdom of God is properly employed by us to bless God's creation. This is why we must hear wisdom and become doers – exercising the power of God. The anointing grows when we receive the wisdom of God and exercise that wisdom. For instance, the Bible says that we are the head and not the tail – this is wisdom. But putting this wisdom into action will only become possible when we sit down to analyze our lives to know if we have actually become the head – increasing in all that we do. The anointing shrinks with the wisdom of the world but the word of God and the revelations we have as we become closer to Him increase the anointing, so that our exploits bring success always. This will readily be noticed in our relationships with children. If you are the type who loves little children, and they easily comes around you, then you will definitely succeed in life.

Now that the Order has found one who has been Anointed to carry out the dictates and decrees of the Order, he/she would only be rewarded depending on how many children of God are restored back to their rightful place in God through the dissemination of spiritual secrets from the Order into the earth in order to institute the heart of God on earth. As the prophet Isaiah instructed: *Ye shall defile also the covering of thy graven images of silver, and the ornament of thy molten images of gold: thou shalt cast them away as a menstruous cloth; thou shalt say unto it, Get thee hence. Then shall he give the rain of thy seed, that thou shalt sow the ground withal; and bread of the increase of the earth, and it shall be fat and plenteous: in that day shall thy cattle feed in large pastures.* – Isaiah 30:22-23.

The Anointed knows that the only way the earth will see the blessings and favour of God is for the earth and the inhabitants to create the atmosphere that will attract His presence. Naturally, the earth is designed by God to manufacture nutrients through biological and chemical means. Human interaction with the earth has polluted the environment to the extent that plants and animals alike are dying by the day. The devil has also led the hearts of men to appreciate evil manipulative tendencies so that men love the world – sports, money, women, pleasure, travel, etc. We are going to go into the Bible to discuss the achievements of these Anointed of God.

The anointing is for work. The reason we don't succeed is because of the mistakes we make daily. This is why the Bible says in Psalms 23:3 that God had to restore the soul of the Anointed before he would be Anointed, and that he would begin to experience exploits thereafter. This would mean repentance and accepting Jesus as your Lord and saviour, seeking the anointing; the oil to attract the Holy Spirit, and then the Angels would come to take your prayers to God and also minister to you in order to bring you abundant increase. We all need the anointing to move on. This is why Matthew 6:33 says that not until one seeks the kingdom of God, meaning, doing the will of the Order, will he or she experience increase, which the Bible refers to as, 'all these things shall follow you'. When you don't believe in God – when you are not filled with His wisdom to increase Faith in the things of the Order - then you can't claim to be *for* God. Your exploits will be achieved when you become established in the world. And since your exploits have to be announced, you will also need to start preparing how to manage the announcement that will come with the announcement the anointing is giving you. Failure to do this may mean that you will not stay long on the mountain of success.

The 'Anointed' walks under the bidding of a voice - Isaiah 30:21: *And thine ears shall hear a word behind thee, saying, This is the way, walk ye in it, when ye turn to the right hand, and when ye turn to the left.* That voice is the voice of God and the voice must be spoken to the Anointed in due season - as we encounter obstacles in life or problems challenging our responsibilities, as agreed by the Order: The Anointed relies on the teachings of the Holy spirit: *But the Comforter, which is the Holy Ghost, whom the Father will send in my name, he shall teach you all things, and bring all things to your remembrance, whatsoever I have said unto you.* - John 14:26. This is what the Psalmist meant by: *He restoreth my soul: he leadeth me in the paths of righteousness for his name's sake.* - Psalms 23:3. The Anointed employs the tools God has given him as wisdom from the Order to pull down the devil's strongholds in the lives of the children of God.

Let's go back to the basics. In Genesis 1:1-2, the heavens and earth were created. The earth was in pain, heaven was in glory. God had to send His Holy Spirit to go before His voice so that the earth would receive life. So the purpose of God's spirit, sent from the anointing Order, is to put things right. We see this in St. Paul's statement in 1 Corinthians 13:1-2, where he talked about the gifts of the spirit and how through love these gifts can help improve the quality of lives. The Anointed is an instrument the Order uses to put things right. This is why, when the Anointed is in authority, in whichever capacity, the people rejoice (Proverbs 29:2). Our understanding of the purpose of the Order's need of restoration will make us ensure that every profession on earth must be carried out in line with the Order's requirements, and everyone who works to earn a living, including inventors, must seek the anointing of the Melchizedek Order so that they can add value to society and church.

The pains we have in the world today have been created by the devil's subtle nature, which he fuses into the heart of man so that man would disobey every instruction form the Anointing Order.

Now, the devil was cast out from heaven to experience pain on earth for the following reasons, which we can find in Jesus' rebuke of the devil:

- *Man shall not live by bread alone* - Matthew 4:4. This is where the distraction comes from. Remember He just fasted and was hungry. But Jesus desired more than just food. His light was about to shine so that God would receive glory, and all He needed was the voice from God to tell Him which way to walk: ...*but every word that proceeds from the mouth of God.* Jesus knew what He was expecting - the fullness of the Holy Spirit so that the Godhead would be complete in Him.

- *Thou shall not tempt God* - Matthew 4:7. The moment you lack faith in God, you begin to tempt Him. When you tempt God you will miss His help. This was the problem with Satan, he tempted God in heaven by murmuring in heaven. Jesus knew that to see success, you must believe every word of God that comes into your heart and move ahead to do what the word says - action is all you need once you hear the voice from the Order speaking behind you.

■ 'Get ye behind me Satan' (Matthew 4:10). You must cast out every voice of opposition in you. Every voice that speaks failure must go behind you. This is how achievements come. The voice of Satan is the voice of pain. He makes you take a long route through pain and complaints. If you do not cast him out, you will begin to believe there is no easy way out of the predicament you are experiencing. And what you would have spent one day on, you end up spending months on because of lack of focus and constant distractions that the devil pushes forward, ahead of you.

Jesus says: ... *only the Lord thy God, and him only shalt thou worship*. The initiation and continuity of exploits reside in the principle of worship - focusing on the Lamb on the throne the author and finisher of your faith. As you worship God in truth and spirit today, I see your exploits manifesting.

What then are exploits?

■ Announcement
■ Establishment
■ Profit

- Success
- Influence
- Good health
- Fruitfulness
- Joy unspeakable
- Peace
- Beauty

All these lead to what I would term unprecedented achievements.

It has become necessary to have a deeper understanding of the elemental entities of the Melchizedek Order. This revelation came to me upon my bed on the 25th July 2012. The Order came into existence without a beginning, seen in the physical as a cloudy mass. King David says of God: 'He makes the clouds his chariot and rides on the wings of the wind' - Psalms 104:3. This was why the Bible also said that Jesus was received by a cloud – Acts 1:9. Then the Order created the Heavens and the Earth, and by default resided in Heaven. Because of the role the earth would play later in the entire purpose of the Order, the Holy Spirit left Heaven. This was the first time the Order visited Earth with a duty to investigate and sanctify the Earth so that it could be incubated with the thoughts of the Order, and then bring forth the desires of the Order.

To ensure that these desires were established and not removed, the Order created a Garden of Eden to house the agent of the Order who would eventually oversee all that the Order had desired in place. From thence, we have the preparatory process to have an extension of the Order here on Earth.

When God planted the garden of Eden, He used the angels to put the garden in place and Lucifer planted the seed of good and evil in the middle of the Garden because of the pride in his heart, which finally became the tree of the knowledge of good and evil. Hence God warned Adam not to eat from it because it was the tree planted by the devil to cause havoc in the Garden so that man would not be in God's presence. That tree planted by the devil, which is the only reason he attracted Eve to the tree, can be likened to the tares sown by the evil one when the good man was as sleep – Matthew 13:24-26: *Another parable put he forth unto them, saying, The kingdom of heaven is likened unto a man which sowed good seed in his field: But while men slept, his enemy came and sowed tares among the wheat, and went his way. But when the blade was sprung up, and brought forth fruit, then appeared the tares also.* This was exactly what the devil did in that garden – he planted that seed that produced the fruit of good and evil. The tree would produce fruits that would be irresistible, just like the beauty of Lucifer, the planter. It was after the fall of man that the Order decided that every tree not approved by the Father would be uprooted (Matthew 15:13), yet for an appointed time.

Allowing the man to taste the fruit of life would have caused havoc to mankind, as there wouldn't have been any means to rescue the man through the death of Christ, because he would have lived forever in evil. The knowledge of evil was a default for the world, which was already experiencing darkness before God spoke light into it. The way the earth received supernatural illumination after the Holy Spirit had hovered around it is the same way we would be delivered from destruction only after the Holy Spirit had sanctified us.

The following entities are wombs for conceiving what the Order would want to manifest in the physical which would become the purpose of the Order for mankind. It all started from the days of creation, and a look at the Garden of Eden would tell of what the Order needs to make life bearable for everyone to live on earth. Now, we would be seeing the following Bible verses to enable us explain in detail what these entities are in the physical and how they would enable us to picture clearly what the Order represents, through the principle of understanding the unknown through the known, which over time has been the principle of creative imagination. I have decided to use the NIV translation of the Bible for the purpose of reading clarity:

■ The Anointed's Vision

1. **'I looked, and I saw a** *windstorm* **coming out of the north— an immense** *cloud* **with** *flashing lightning* **and surrounded by** *brilliant light.* **The centre of the** *fire* **looked like** *glowing metal'* – Ezekiel 1:4. Here we would see the following entities – windstorm, cloud, lightening, light, fire and glowing metal. In visions I have also seen these entities.

2. **'Then the Spirit lifted me up, and I heard behind me a loud** *rumbling sound* **- May the glory of the Lord be praised in his dwelling place! The sound of the wings of the living creatures brushing against each other and the sound of the wheels beside them, a loud rumbling sound.'** – Ezekiel 3:12:13. Here, Ezekiel heard the sound of praise only when he was in the spirit. This is why a music minister in the church who does not have the spirit of God in him/her can never lead a spirit-filled worship and praise session in the church because he/she will not be able to replicate the Order values on earth, enabling the kingdom of God to come on earth. Every spirit filled worship sound of musical instruments attracts the attention of the Order. Our human spirit also responds in like manner. Good melodious sound is food for the human spirit. Heavy and fast paced sound energises our spirit. In most cases people faint when they hear heavy crashing sound like in an accident and the human spirit would leave

the body until such a time when there is calmness for it to return. The understanding that the spirit can return is the hope of raising the dead back to life. When the Anointed is in a scene where God would use him to raise the dead, he is transformed by the Order into a realm where he would see the human spirit floating and then descending and entering into the lifeless body.

■ How the Anointed uses physical creations of the Order: *For the invisible things of him from the creation of the world are clearly seen, being understood by the things that are made, even his eternal power and Godhead; so that they are without excuse: -* Romans 1:20.

1. **The Earth** – The earth is the footstool of God and represents a solid base for the support of life Man was created from the earth. It grows the forests, which is the habitat for the beasts of the field. So the Anointed mentions the earth in prayers that has to do with increase or abundant life. For instance: '*You are the salt of the earth...*' (Matthew 5:13). The Anointed could pick up grains of sand and decree increase. Knowing that the earth grows whatever is sown into it, he could also write his heart's desires on a piece of paper, bury it in the earth, keep watering the spot and pray for increase. When we

were building the church and there seemed to be no funds, I took some few notes of money, buried them in the land. I had to command the land to produce the money we needed to build on it, and in less than two years we were through.

2. **The Waters** – The Garden of Eden was circumscribed by waters. The earth came out of the waters. And the rain comes to water the earth. Man lives between waters – down on the earth and up in the sky. Scripture made several references to water as representing the presence of God – *fountain of living waters, rivers of joy, rivers of living water, rivers in the desert, the beam of God's chambers in the waters,* etc. Without water there would be no life on earth – drinking, bathing, growing plants and rearing fish. So the Anointed uses his scriptural understanding of water as the origin of all creations to decree things to past. He can sprinkle water on anything and decree it to receive life – be it business, someone who is sick, general prayers of peace, etc.

3. **The Sky** – The stars, sun, and moon are all entities living in the sky. They represent eternity in the eyes and the hearts of the Anointed. This is why the Anointed prays looking up to the sky. Abraham was told by God to look

upon the stars to enable him to understand his increase. The Anointed uses such instances that abound in the Bible to speak life into his own life – business, ministry, illness, etc – and he sees results. This act of the Anointed is what many refer to as the act of prophecy.

4. **The Clouds** – The clouds are referred to as the 'chariots of God' by David in Psalms 104: 3-4. We would see that the clouds are always in motion, and they gather to bring rain upon the earth. The Anointed could use this understanding to pray thus – ' as the clouds gather, so would my prayers gather before the throne of God to bring me rain of abundance.' Or he could pray thus – 'as long as the clouds keep moving, I will never experience stagnation all the days of my life.'

5. **The Wind** – The Bible made reference to wind as bringing God's power into play – blessing or punishment. The Bible in Psalms 104: 4 says that God moves upon the wings of the wind. So the Anointed can pray thus – 'O Lord! Set me upon the wings of your wind and take me to the destination of my peace.' He could also stay in the wind, raising his hands towards heaven and praying – 'I cast my burden in this wind and I receive peace in return.'

6. **The Air**: The air we breathe is the essence of the life we have. God breathed into Adam and He became a living soul. Jesus breathed upon His disciples and commanded them to receive the Holy Spirit. So the Anointed uses this premise as the basis to breathe on the dead or sick and command life into them and it would be so.

7. **Sound** - The thunders from heaven are a different manifestation of the Order upon earth. The Bible talks of trumpets that brought down the walls of Jericho. This experience never fades out of the mind of the Anointed. The waterfalls, the sea's roar, the cry of children, sounds made by animals, etc, are evidence of the existence of God. The Anointed uses sound in his communication with the Order in worship and songs of praise. Musical instruments make sounds to add beauty to the service of man to God. I woke up one morning with a song on my lips, resounding as I woke up from sleep to life and the lyrics read:

I can hear the song of Praise
Singing Hallelujah
To the Lamb on the throne
I can hear the beat of salvation
Right in my heart
As you dwell in me, Jesus.

This song reassures me of His presence in my life, giving me the assurance of life and the supporting arm of God in my ministry. This is one way the Anointed knows that God is still with him/her. In his prayers, he could make references to the sound of a creation of God which he wants replicated in his life, for instance, he could say – 'Lord! I want to hear the cry of a baby in this house before this time next year.' Or in a more definitive way, he could say – 'I decree, before this time next year, the cry of a child will be heard in this house.' He knows exactly what he expects to see – a living child and not a dead child.

8. **Fire** – The Order appeared as a fire in the burning bush. And in the book of Acts chapter 2 the Bible says that there was a cloven tongue of fire upon the disciples. The Anointed uses this phenomenon of fire to explain what he expects to see in certain situations.

9. **Light** – This is evident from what God created first. And after the existence of light everything fell into place. The Anointed with the heart of exploits uses light as an instrument of release. He may pray – 'I decree light into your life from today.'

10. **Numbers** - Several pieces of evidence in the Bible show

that numbers are instruments of prophetic decrees used by the Anointed.

What the Anointed does is to replicate what he hears or sees in the spirit realm in the physical, and he will see results. Are you Anointed? It is time to decree things to pass.

CHAPTER SIX

THE ANOINTING CHARACTER

In the discussion that follows we will be discussing what makes the Anointed to work the way he does. In trying to find an easy way out of every situation, he works with the following facts in the Bible:

1. God is love and therefore loves him – John 3:16.
2. God has prepared an inheritance for him and has also set His angels to protect it – Psalms 16:5.
3. The lines falls in pleasant places if he is in right standing with God and would not need to struggle to succeed – Psalms 16:6.
4. The angels are in charge of his inheritance and also knows the path that leads to it – Exodus 23:20.
5. The angels are easily angered by man's imperfection because they are holy – Exodus 23:20.
6. In the presence of God there is fullness of Joy – Psalm 16:11.

7. When God was in heaven, we are told that our words should be few (Ecclesiastes 5:2). Now that God is with us (Emmanuel), our words should therefore be fewer – implying that God will only answer heartfelt desires devoid of greed, injustice and unrighteousness. It is now more of spirit to spirit communication, deep calling unto deep.

8. Without the spirit of Christ in him, he can do nothing – John 15:5, Galatians 4:6.

9. Those who know their God shall possess unimaginable strength with which they would do exploits – and he sets his heart to know God, Daniel 11:32b.

10. 'My people suffer for lack of knowledge (Hosea 4:6),' is God's concern, so the Anointed seeks to have more knowledge of what he sees daily, understanding his surroundings.

The Anointing Character explains what the anointing is supposed to achieve. Earlier we explained how those Anointed to work in God's vineyard were called and how they succeeded. For instance, we saw that Moses was humble - a character that came to be in him as he lived with his in-laws, tending his flocks for a period of forty years. This was the characteristic that enabled him to succeed. Humility does not come except by learning to accept yourself in every situation you find yourself. We also saw earlier that the woman was created with some character in her which should enable her to be able to perform the duty of 'help' that God created her for. We have heard of federal character. Wherever the Anointed is, the Anointing Character, which represent the intention of the Order is what brings about his exploits.

One such character is also seen in Matthew 11:12: *And from the days of John the Baptist until now the kingdom of heaven suffereth violence, and the violent take it by force.* We would see the Anointing Character embedded in the verse - *the violent take it by force.* What violence did the kingdom suffer in the hands of men? Injustice and depopulation of the kingdom as souls were perishing daily for lack of knowledge. So the Anointing Character would be; an aggressive soul wining through preaching and teaching of the word everywhere, casting out of demons from those possessed, making authorities in power to respect justice especially for widows and the poor among us, among other avenues to improve the quality of life the people lives through the use of the power from the Order.

How the Anointed works
He relies on wisdom to live on earth, knowing that the world is being ruled by the devil – Revelations 12:9-12. How did he get this knowledge and his reliance on the wisdom of God, to

enable him to succeed? Wisdom sits on seven pillars (Proverbs 9:1), which are the seven spirits of God – Spirit of the Lord, knowledge, might, understanding, etc. Wisdom makes one see beyond today. A man with the wisdom of God will know how to use the verses of the Bible to beautify his life and know exactly what to do when the need arises. The book of Revelation 13:18 says: 'Here is wisdom. Let him that hath understanding count the number of the beast: for it is the number of a man; and his number is six hundred threescore and six.'

Wisdom leads us into the world of understanding as we begin to receive insights into what God is saying to our spirit. Many believe that this will be physically marked in people. But this refers to world leadership authority ruling with the devil's wisdom so that the world will be controlled by some sets of promulgations that will make it difficult for the righteous to do business, just as people join cults, lie, cheat, etc in order to succeed in life. We will see why the Anointed relies so much on the power of wisdom below:

- Those who succeed speak wisdom because their hearts utters understanding- Psalms 49:3
- From every verse of Scripture he studies he filters out the wisdom therein and uses it to better his life and those of others to please God. This act of his enables him to depend on the word of God, for all he does.

- He is willing and ready to teach the word of God so that more people can get filled with the wisdom of God - 2 Timothy 2:2

- The Anointed understand the hidden wisdom that is required to live an abundant life on earth - 1 Corinthians 2:7

- He relies on the spirit of Christ crying in his heart as the source of the strength and wisdom - Galatians 4:6

- If God uses him as a pastor, he knows that he has to feed God's children with knowledge and understanding - Jeremiah 3:15

- He understands that God's ultimate concern is how He might dwell in the heart of His children - Jeremiah 31:31-34

- He goes back to meet God all the time to get direction – Isaiah 1:18

- He knows that the only way to succeed is to be willing and obedient to God's wisdom so that he will not be put to shame – Isaiah 1:19, Jeremiah 8:9

- In doing all these, his heart yearns for growth, physically and spiritually – Luke 2:40, 52; 3 John 1:2

- To ensure that he experiences prosperity, he takes the command of the Lord into heart – Deuteronomy 28

In Isaiah 30:21 we saw that the word of God is the tool needed by the Anointed to function. We have gone through how Jesus defeated the devil in Matthew 4. We all receive wages for our work. Amen. There is dignity in labour. Dignity is exploits. You become respected because you are dignified. If you are serving God without a reward that dignifies you, then you are either not Anointed, you are Anointed and do not know it, or you do not know how to use the anointing. Many of us had been Anointed before by servants of God yet, how many of us are benefiting from that anointing? Being born again means rejecting our yesterday, which was filled with woes, and accepting our today, which we hope to be fruitful in God.

For every work the Anointed does, he gets paid by God. So what he does is to see how he can touch the heart of the King, in line with what the Order decrees, so that the King will release for him. To do this he tries to understand how Jesus worked here on earth, because Jesus came to teach us how to work to earn God's favour. Jesus says He does what the father does. He replied to Philip that those who know Him know God. So, there is no need to look for God if you know Jesus. He even said that the kingdom must come before we can do the will of God here on earth while teaching the Lord's Prayer. The kingdom is here already, for He preached saying: repent, for the kingdom of God is at hand – here, meaning that the Melchizedek Order is life with us here on earth.

So now the Anointed knows that all he need do is to

follow the will of God, and this is possible when the spirit of Christ cries in his heart. Then he goes back to pray for the release of the Holy Spirit upon him, because Jesus told us that the anointing is upon Him to do exploits – Luke 4:18. Not until we have the Spirit of God, which is the mind of God in us, may we hear messages from the Order. The Bible says that whoever has the Holy Spirit living in him/her will also experience an overshadowing effect of the power of God: *The Holy Ghost shall come upon thee, and the power of the Highest shall overshadow thee* – Luke 1:35. An instance is seen in Ezekiel 2:2: *As he spoke, the Spirit came into me and raised me to my feet, and I heard him speaking to me* (NIV). Not until the spirit came into Ezekiel did he hear what the Order was speaking to him. Taking lessons from Acts 1:8, the Anointed clearly looks at the content of whatever instruction the Order releases, and outlines his duties to merit God's reward. For instance, let's see what the Order told Ezekiel: *He said: 'Son of man, I am sending you to the Israelites, to a rebellious nation that has rebelled against me; they and their fathers have been in revolt against me to this very day. The people to whom I am sending you are obstinate and stubborn. Say to them, 'This is what the Sovereign Lord says.* – Ezekiel 2:3-4 (NIV). The Order will also tell the Anointed the challenges he will face ahead: *And whether they listen or fail to listen for they are a rebellious house - they will know that a prophet has been among them. And you, son of man, do not be afraid of them or their words. Do not be afraid, though briers and thorns are all around you and you live among scorpions. Do not be afraid of what they say or terrified by them, though they are a rebellious house. You must speak my words to them, whether they listen or fail to listen, for they are rebellious'* Ezekiel 2:5-7 (NIV). In my case the Order said: 'I am sending you to the church – my children are scattered and they do not know where they are going. Recruit, train and spiritually empower them with the wisdom to execute my will on earth. They will, however not listen to you, but I am raising you as a testimony against them.' This somehow is a resemblance of what God told Ezekiel: *... for I have made you a sign to the house of Israel -* Ezekiel 12:6 (NIV). And later in another vision, I heard: *'Now they have despised you and the word I sent you to speak to them, they will henceforth stretch forth their hands and I will punch them with holes so that their blessings will leak through, concentrate and write the books, many are here to distract you, but be focus and write the books.'* This was how I received the spirit and strength that is helping me to write the books with so much ease and such deep scriptural insights. God releases a confrontational strength to you the moment you have the Anointing: *But I will make you as unyielding and hardened as they are –* Ezekiel 3:8 (NIV). People have asked me where I get the strength to write from – it is the Anointing. The Anointing makes the difference, and this is why I am here revealing this secret to you so that you would seek the anointing of the Order and live a fruitful life, excelling above your peers as it happened to Daniel: *Then this Daniel was preferred above the presidents and princes, because an excellent spirit was in him; and the king thought to set him over the whole realm* – Daniel 6:3.

The Holy Spirit is the agent of the kingdom of God, the Order of Melchizedek, here on earth, from the wisdom we got in the Lord's Prayer and the release of the Holy Spirit in Acts 2. The will of God that must be done on earth is the 'vision of God' for this earth and we can see His heart desire for this earth in Genesis 1:1-27.

The Anointed looks into John 3:1-5. He knows that one must see the kingdom before he/she will enter. And to enter means that he/she is filled with the Holy Spirit. Once he starts to receive wisdom from the Order, he starts applying them, as he is not suppose to be a hearer only, imitating Jesus - and he gets a reward.

Every king rewards those who obey his instructions to the letter. Those who disobey are ostracized to ensure there are no more rebels, because to obey is better than to plead for forgiveness. This is the rule that governs the Anointing Order.

So he goes to filter out what God hates in the Bible and promises not to do it. God hears his heartbeat and starts watching him. He also knows that by strength alone shall no man prevail, so he calls on Jesus to help him along the path of perfection down which God is leading him – the path of the Order. And from time to time he checks his conscience, because that is what condemns us first. Any time he gets a condemnation, he tries to repent, pleading for forgiveness.

Then he tells others his testimonies in order to win more souls to God through Jesus, who is championing this rescue mission. Heaven rejoices seeing the new soul, then the worker that brought in that soul is rewarded. He obtains mercy as he forgives others. He clears his heart so that he can see God instructing him because the pure in heart shall see God – Matthew 5:8. Once he can see God, which is the presence of the Order in his heart, then he can receive Melchizedical illumination, which enables the Anointed to live a worthy life: *To the pure, all things are pure, but to those who are corrupted and do not believe, nothing is pure. In fact, both their minds and consciences are corrupted.* - Titus 1:15 (NIV)

He looks at Jesus' command that we should leave our relations and friends to serve Him. He checks the meaning to imply that we should abandon the wisdom we had received from these close relatives of ours who share the same burden of pains with us - remember his own people mocked him because they were his relatives. Their stories of generational failures, barrenness, near success, should be detested. Just follow the light Jesus stands for.

Now let's see how Jesus operated with the authority from the Anointing Order:

- He speaks, because the words have the power to cause the change we expect - John 5:8-10: *Jesus saith unto him, Rise, take up thy bed, and walk. And immediately the man was made whole, and took up his bed, and walked: and on the same day was the sabbath. The Jews therefore said unto him that was cured, ...*

- He preached the message of repentance – Matthew 4:17: *From that time on Jesus began to preach, 'Repent, for the kingdom of heaven is near.'*

- Jesus also taught in the temple, correcting wrong practices – Luke 19:47 (NIV): *Every day he was teaching at the temple.* I don't support the belief in some Christian circles that we cannot only function in distinct gifts. I know Jesus did all things to the glory of God using the gifts of healing, prophecy, teaching, preaching, welfare service, etc. if you desire a specific anointing, go for it – the Lord will in no wise cast away your request – ask and you shall receive; this is the word of promise from Jesus – He cannot lie. As the Bible says: *For no matter how many promises God has made, they are 'Yes' in Christ. And so through him the 'Amen' is spoken by us to the glory of God.* – 2 Corinthians 1:20 (NIV).

- Jesus prayed on several occasions, especially in the night on the Mount of Olives – John17:1-2 (NIV): *After Jesus said this, he looked toward heaven and prayed: 'Father, the time has come. Glorify your Son, that your Son may glorify you. For you granted him authority over all people that he might give eternal life to all those you have given him.* Now, you would see that He referred to the intention of the Order – the authoritative presence of God on earth so as to turn every vessel of shame, which the devil had mutilated with worldly wisdom, into a vessel of honour unto Him.

■ He was obedient to the call of God – Luke 2:49 (NIV): *Why were you searching for me?' he asked. 'Didn't you know I had to be in my Father's house?'*

So the Anointed just go ahead and do these things, building on the existing foundation Christ had raised, and God rewards the Anointed accordingly: *For no one can lay any foundation other than the one already laid, which is Jesus Christ.* – 1 Corinthians 3:11.

How will the Anointed speak like Jesus? How will he speak into life? It is by following the instruction in Romans 12:2: *And be not conformed to this world: but be ye transformed by the renewing of your mind, that ye may prove what is that good, and acceptable, and perfect, will of God.* Now let's see how this transformation process can be - John 3:1-5: *There was a man of the Pharisees, named Nicodemus, a ruler of the Jews: The same came to Jesus by night, and said unto him, Rabbi, we know that thou art a teacher come from God: for no man can do these miracles that thou doest, except God be with him. Jesus answered and said unto him, Verily, verily, I say unto thee, except a man be born again, he cannot see the kingdom of God. Nicodemus saith unto him, how can a man be born when he is old? Can he enter the second time into his mother's womb, and be born? Jesus answered, Verily, verily, I say unto thee, Except a man be born of water and of the Spirit, he cannot enter into the kingdom of God.*

The first term there is 'Born again.' What then is born again? It simply means renewing our mind, so that it may beat with the pulsating codes from the Order. Even if you have been failing, clear that thought of failure from your mind. That is the born- again process. A new-born child learns to become either a success or a failure in life, depending on many factors – the prevailing environmental wisdom which he imbibes daily, the mentors he admires, his own determination, etc. We would say that to be Born Again means to clear your mind and become like a new child with no prior knowledge of the world.

The second compound term there is 'Born of water and of the Spirit.' This means to be filled with the wisdom, knowledge and understanding of God. Here, the Holy Spirit teaches you, and you apply the wisdom for exploits - John 7:38: *He that believeth in me, as the scripture hath said, out of his belly shall flow rivers of living water.*

So when this wisdom starts to flow because you have been filled with heavenly wisdom, you will know how to speak like God does, in accordance with the Order's intention of Restoration - Matthew 5:48: *Be ye therefore perfect, even as your Father which is in heaven is perfect.*

When you speak like God, what you say becomes perfected just as God did it in the beginning. This is how your exploit would start – turning every ugly situation around you and in your life into the form that will represent the perfect will of God, as seen in the beauty in the flowers of the garden.

The Anointed calls the name Jesus and he decrees a thing with the name and power to come down to put things in order. The Anointed speaks - only speaks, because he knows the authority behind him, who is greater than the devil and all his demons put together – Acts 18:9-10: *One night the Lord spoke to Paul in a vision: 'Do not be afraid; keep on speaking, do not be silent. For I am with you, and no one is going to attack and harm you,...(NIV).* The Melchizedical Order illumination in the heart of the Anointed is perfected in John 14:12-14: *Verily, verily, I say unto you, He that believeth on me, the works that I do shall he do also; and greater works than these shall he do; because I go unto my Father. And whatsoever ye shall ask in my name, that will I do, that the Father may be glorified in the Son. If ye shall ask any thing in my name, I will do it.*

What is the meaning of 'in Jesus' Name?' Can one ever be

able to mention that name without knowing Him? You know Him, that is why you can call His name. How can you know Him when He has not been shown to you? Now you will know. Christ is wisdom, as shown in the following Bible verses:

- Luke 2:40 – 'And the child grew, and waxed strong in spirit, filled with wisdom: and the grace of God was upon him.'

- Luke 11:49 – 'Therefore also said the wisdom of God, I will send them prophets and apostles [*from the Anointing Order*], and some of them they shall slay and persecute:' (emphasis mine).

- 1 Corinthians 1:24 – 'But unto them which are called, both Jews and Greeks, Christ the power of God, and the wisdom of God.'

So when you say 'in Jesus' name', you are calling the power and wisdom of God into action. This means you must know Jesus in and out, as the disciples knew Him because they had been with Him. The word of God is that key to unlock your knowledge of God. That is why you are reading this book, so that when you call on that name He will answer and you will receive Power and Wisdom to come out of your predicament. St. Paul says: 'For the Jews require a sign, and the Greeks seek after wisdom [*worldly wisdom; astrology, science, archeology, etc*]: But we preach Christ crucified, unto the Jews a stumbling block, and unto the Greeks foolishness.' (*Emphasis mine*).

Many the world over are busy looking for signs and miracles, while others are looking for scientific or archaeological proofs before they can accept the restoration order of the Anointing Order. So the name of Jesus has become a stumbling block and foolishness to these sets of people, because they lack the faith to unleash the power the name bears. Even at this, there was still a disciple from both nations mentioned above who was steadfast in the Lord: ... *a disciple named Timothy lived, whose mother was a Jewess and a believer, but whose father was a Greek* – Acts 16:1(NIV). This is what is making it difficult for many of us to talk with God. We are told in the Bible: Blessed are those who believe yet have not seen. The Restoration process is made easy by God through preaching, so that we would be admitted into the Anointing Order – 1 Corinthians 1:21: *For after that in the wisdom of God the world by wisdom knew not God, it pleased God by the foolishness of preaching to save them that believe*. But overtime, the world has gone after *worldly wisdom; astrology, science, archeology, etc*, to find solution to every problem in the world. The Anointing Order does not necessarily work signs because signs manifests in whoever the Order admits to be a bearer of divine wisdom as it happens to King Solomon. The greatest sign and miracle that anyone should thirst after is the possession by the Holy Spirit. The Order lives on divine wisdom.

The only strength Joshua had was the spirit of wisdom

(Deuteronomy 34:9) and with this he became successful as a leader. The power of God comes with great terror, and the people will become terrified - Deuteronomy 34:12.

Power leads to the manifestation of miracles, but wisdom helps you to sustain miracles. When you receive a miracle and refuse to grow in the wisdom of God, you will not know how to serve and revere God and before you know it, your miracle fades out of reality because you won't know when you will fall into sin. Miracles are possible through a spiritual transformation that takes place within seconds in some cases, and to sustain the miracle in your life, you must be answerable at all times to the spiritual authority that instituted that miracle in your life, because as it is, that condition belongs to that spiritual Order.

If people are aware of the implications of miracles, they will not go after them. They would rather chose to receive divine wisdom from the Anointing Order. The wisdom of God helps you to know what, how and when to pray.

The power and wisdom of God are tools for evangelism. At the mention of the name Jesus power comes down, and those who see and experience this power will give thanks to God by confessing Him as Lord - meaning that the moment they receive the power, they will begin to win souls by pointing them to Jesus. Wisdom comes with power (1 Corinthians 1:24). No power, No exploit. Wealth comes through wisdom. No exploit, No wealth. They all go hand in hand, pouring out through that same windows of heaven referred to in Malachi 3:10. This is why in Romans 11:33 the Bible says: *O the depth of the riches both of the wisdom and knowledge of God! how unsearchable are his judgments, and his ways past finding out!*

Exploits involve giving something in your life to God. Knowing what to give, when to give, where to give, how to give, matters a lot, and to a large extent would define your level of increase in life: *A son honoureth his father, and a servant his master: if then I be a father, where is mine honour? and if I be a master, where is my fear? saith the Lord of hosts... And if ye offer the blind for sacrifice, is it not evil? and if ye offer the lame and sick, is it not evil? offer it now unto thy governor; will he be pleased with thee, or accept thy person? - Malachi 1:6, 8.*

How The Anointed Think

Now, see how the Anointed think 'there is an easy way out.' That is what He thinks daily: 'Oh God grant me the wisdom to know this easy way out, give me the knowledge to apply and the understanding thereof.' This was the expectation of the disciples as they waited on Jesus to teach them how to pray. This was also the expectation of Solomon as he waited on God to grant him wisdom. A time came when Elijah had to go to Horeb to see God, but Jesus lived with us here on earth, and today one does not have to go to Horeb to seek the face of God. The Order allows for negotiation as would be seen in Abraham's discussion with the angels. So the Anointed goes ahead to negotiate his terms with the Order through prayers and waits for their response.

The Anointed does not accept disappointment. He is a resilient fellow, believing that some day his request will be answered. His joy is in the testimonies he will soon share. He doesn't give up – that is the heart of the Anointed. This is why he keeps on going back to the Order. He starts his prayers and requests to God with the statement: *if I found favour in your sight*. A time came when God told Moses to strike the rock with his staff, and on another occasion when he would have done the same, God told him to speak. There is always another way out. Because someone is undergoing 40 days' fasting to get his/her breakthrough does not mean you must do the same to get out of a predicament.

Those who want to fight the devil should know that he works on people's intelligence through wisdom and knowledge. The devil tempted Jesus and showed him all the allures of this world, but Christ declined to be moved into appreciating worldliness. So anyone who would wear jewellery or love man's wisdom should be prepared for the devil.

The only way to win spiritual warfare is to avoid what attracts the devil's attention – jewels and unworthy travels that waste our time and money because the devil moves to and fro, meaning he is a traveller without a plan, cursing people, wicked acts, etc. Only when the devil leaves you will your prayers be answered: *Then the devil leaveth him, and, behold, angels came and ministered unto him* – Matthew 4:11. We are told that out of the eater came out something to eat – but before this happened, the eater had to be killed through the bravery act of Samson. The enemy in you must die before you can experience peace. This is why the Bible says that we should flee from every appearance of evil. If we do this we see that we do not have to battle with the devil. We would only go ahead and teach people about the wisdom of God and how to make God happy through our acts of righteousness. And when we do this, our God will surely stand to defend us by raising up a standard against the enemy. What we have done is to leave what we are supposed to do and take over what is the work of God, fighting battles that God would fight on our behalf.

We can get an insight from Ecclesiastes 10:10: ... *but wisdom is profitable to direct.* All you need is wisdom. If you don't have what it takes to succeed in life, ask God for wisdom. Solomon did not have what it takes; he met God for wisdom.

Another source of illumination for the Anointed is found in Exodus 31:1-5: *And the Lord spake unto Moses, saying, See, I have called by name Bezaleel the son of Uri, the son of Hur, of the tribe of Judah: And I have filled him with the spirit of God, in wisdom, and in understanding, and in knowledge, and in all manner of workmanship, To devise cunning works, to work in gold, and in silver, and in brass, And in cutting of stones, to set them, and in carving of timber, to work in all manner of workmanship.* This confirms that admission into the Melchizedek Anointing Order is for the purpose of filling one with the wisdom, understanding and knowledge that will make them execute the will of God on Earth, which will enable all men to come to know Him as their God, through the testimonial manifestations of their handiworks.

It is time to ask God for the gift of wisdom – say 'God, make me more like Jesus'. He has answered. The name Jesus will bring the power and wisdom of God into your life so that: *When men are cast down, then thou shalt say, There is lifting up; and he shall save the humble person.* – Job 22:29.

123

CHAPTER SEVEN

QUALITIES OF THE ANOINTED

So far we have talked about tools needed by the Anointed – in Isaiah 30:21, he hears a voice behind which leads the Anointed through the paths of righteousness, as instituted by the Order (Psalms 23:3). We have also discussed how the Anointed works. He puts what he hears into action, and goes ahead to act in line with the spoken word in his strength and might, believing strongly that what he has spoken has taken effect in line with Biblical statements of fact: *Therefore I tell you, whatever you ask for in prayer, believe that you have received it, and it will be yours, Thou shalt also decree a thing, and it shall be established unto thee: and the light shall shine upon thy ways. -* Mark 11:24, Job 22:28.

In this chapter we will be talking of the qualities of the Anointed. These qualities are inborn in the Anointed through the main anointing to enable him fulfill his destiny or purpose in life, as Jesus espoused when He said: ...*To this end was I born, and for this cause came I into the world, that I should bear witness unto the truth.* – Luke 18:37. And what was this cause? Simeon's prophecy tells us: *'Then Simeon blessed them and said to Mary, his mother: 'This child is destined to cause the falling and rising of many in Israel, and to be a sign that will be spoken against, so that the thoughts of many hearts will be revealed. And a sword will pierce your own soul too.'* - Luke 2:34-35 NIV. This is the beauty of the main anointing, which we call destiny. This main anointing receives beauty as we live and interact with the wisdom of God from time to time, in order to take us to God's expected destination for us. The main anointing is what I refer to as being gifted, and the beautification process is what I term as being anointed.

Moses anointed Joshua and that was how He was successful. If God brings you in contact with His servant, know that He wants to develop your anointing, through the hearing of wisdom. You are in contact to help you mend every broken part of your life. We are not in church just to dance and go home, we are here to walk the path of perfection as He promised us church in Isaiah 42:16: *And I will bring the blind by a way that they knew not; I will lead them in paths that they have not known: I will make darkness light before them, and crooked things straight. These things will I do unto them, and not forsake them.*

Why are we talking of these qualities? Our main reason is seen in Matthew 5:48: *Be ye therefore perfect, even as your*

Father which is in heaven is perfect, – meaning our ability to reconcile everyone back to God by treating them as our brothers and sisters, as seen in Matthew 5:46-47: *For if ye love them which love you, what reward have ye? do not even the publicans the same? And if ye salute your brethren only, what do ye more than others? do not even the publicans so?*

We can also see God's standard in John 15:1-5: *I am the true vine, and my Father is the husbandman. Every branch in me that beareth not fruit he taketh away: and every branch that beareth fruit, he purgeth it, that it may bring forth more fruit. Now ye are clean through the word which I have spoken unto you. Abide in me, and I in you. As the branch cannot bear fruit of itself, except it abide in the vine; no more can ye, except ye abide in me. I am the vine, ye are the branches: He that abideth in me, and I in him, the same bringeth forth much fruit: for without me ye can do nothing.*

We all know that Jesus did exactly what God does, and this he achieved because he was Anointed. Who is Jesus? 1 Corinthians 1:24 says who He is: ... *Christ the power of God, and the wisdom of God.* This is implying further as we discussed earlier that anyone who receives the Melchizedek Order anointing will operate in like manner, as Jesus. Implying further that the person who is Anointed to function in the Order must imbibe the character of Jesus which is referred to in this book as the Anointing Character which makes us to become sons of God: *And because ye are sons, God hath sent forth the Spirit of his Son into your hearts, crying, Abba, Father.* – Galatians 4:6. The Bible also gives the reason why one would be Anointed to serve in the Earthly Melchizedek Order – Hebrews 1:9: *You have loved righteousness and hated wickedness; therefore God, your God, has set you above your companions by anointing you with the oil of joy.'* We would see from this that anyone who needs to live the life of joy must be initiated into the Order. The qualities have been summarized to be the *love for righteousness* and this will enable us to have the mind of Christ – 1 Corinthians 2:16: *For who hath known the mind of the Lord, that he may instruct him? But we have the mind of Christ.*

Many of us have what we are presently looking for, but because we don't know that we have it, we have remained where we are today. This is why the Bible says – 1 Corinthians 3:16: *Know ye not that ye are the temple of God, and that the Spirit of God dwelleth in you?* Only when God touches you with His anointing will whatever you do become perfect. You may be a singer without recognition; you need the Holy Spirit to announce you. In Matthew 5:16 Jesus instructed us to shine because this is the character of the Order: *Let your light so shine before men, that they may see your good works, and glorify your Father which is in heaven.* This is simply because God created you for His glory.

To understand the qualities of God, let us go back to basics with God's character as seen through His creative works in Genesis 1:

1. **Ambitious:** God created heaven and earth. Now let us see how big the earth is in all its fullness. Humans, take a look at yourselves. See the animals. These show the ambitious character of the Order. The change of Abram to Abraham shows ambition.

2. **Emotional:** God looked at Adam, and saw that he needed help. Many of us have this emotional quality but use it wrongly - for men who would help a lady and then go to bed with her. A woman interpreting the pretence of emotion for sex does not have the heart of the Order. The angels left heaven to marry the daughters of men because of this emotional quality, which they used wrongly in this wise. Songs from the Anointed will always make you cry. Jesus spoke about His death in an emotionally persuasive manner and the apostles began to be sorrowful, making Him withhold some secrets from them for a while – John 16:12: 'I have yet many things to say unto you, but ye cannot bear them now.' The Anointed can win the hardest of heart with this quality. When they employ this gift in preaching, you see people repenting. This is why they are also passionate and compassionate.

3. **Theocratic in nature**: The Anointed will hardly take wisdom from man because God does not need man's wisdom as input into what He does. All you hear the Anointed say is: *thus saith the Lord*. He only says what God says. They are authoritative leaders, who rely on the authority of God. They are never mediocre – *the violent taketh it by force*. This quality makes him/her a prophet or prophetess.

4. **Teachers**: They are willing and able to teach because God teaches through the Holy Spirit. This is an inherent gift in the Anointed of God as seen in 1 Timothy 3:2. They are the ones who will readily call to teach you in order to impact in you what they have learnt. They derive joy in teaching as David rightly says: *Then I will teach transgressors your ways, and sinners will turn back to you* – Psalm 51:13.

5. **Ambidextrous**: The Anointed have the skill to do several things because of the Spirit of Wisdom, Knowledge and Understanding. They learn easily and find it difficult to have rest until they are through with what they are doing. This ability makes them hardworking. This is why Paul says: 'I can do all things through Christ which strengtheneth' (Philippians 4:13).

6. **Sensitive:** They are sensitive to the situation on the ground. They do not want to make the same mistakes again. They value their integrity and may hate you for lying. They look for the easiest way out of a problem, hence they will often meet you for help - God said, 'let us make man.' It is this same quality that made God get Adam a wife. Jesus also raised disciples to work with him.

7. **Informed:** They are rich in wisdom, knowledge and understanding, which enables them to teach others. They will gather information about anything. Jesus displays this when He fits into every sphere of human knowledge - medicine, law, accounting, engineering etc.

8. **Servant heart:** They are so humble that you hardly know they carry the anointing - they behave more like helpers when you meet them. Jehu's men saw Elisha as a mad man, and Jesus was seen by some as a mere carpenter. Pompous types can't be Anointed by God. They are simple, yet decisive and focused. To pass out faeces we must all strip naked, no matter our class in society. This is what it seems like, to be humble - we give up pride and ego, and allow for the excretion of the wastes in our lives which is the worldly wisdom that we had before we gave our lives to Christ.

9. **Very patient:** They are not the best people to expect quick answers from in most cases. They may seem not to be interested in an issue at the beginning, because they rely on information from the Order before they will speak out. Jesus showed this quality when the woman caught in the very act was brought to Him. He gave them the word and bent down writing. Many of us would have jumped up to save her or even condemn her and make a mockery of her.

10. **Articulate in nature:** They possess a strong sense of maturity in handling issues, due to their articulate nature. They put their words across in such a manner that you cannot say 'no' to them. This is because they work on your emotions. They can easily judge who you are because of the emotional character they display - a character that makes you see them as Help. In arguments, they will defeat you with all the facts vividly presented, and you won't be able to doubt them. Hence they are good researchers, historians, and writers - those who wrote the Bible were all Anointed.

11. **Successful in Business:** Wisdom is the breath of business. The Anointed uses wisdom to put down his business proposals, and because of his/her articulate nature, you will see that you cannot but honour the request.

12. **Possessive:** They don't take their eyes off what is rightly theirs. This makes them good administrators, wives, husbands, fathers, mothers, and anywhere leadership demand is needed. They are ready to defend their possessions. Jesus says in His name we shall cast out demons - this is the Possessive authority. An Anointed man wants to be recognized - Matthew 5:16. This act also makes them jealous, as God is jealous. They can go to any extent to secure what rightfully belongs to them - hence they spend hours convincing God in prayers that He must answer them. If you take anything from a possessive one without his/her consent, then be ready for pursuit.

13. **Resist oppression:** This is in line with their possessive character. Jesus went into the wilderness to be tempted of the devil but when the tempter came, He resisted him. The Bible says we should resist the devil and he will flee. David fought to defend himself and his men. Abraham rescued Lot. The devil was thrown down from heaven. The Anointed resist every form of oppression.

14. **Leadership and Lordship:** This is in line with the character of the Order. Many use this wrongly, being sometimes too autocratic, and seemingly wanting people to always serve them.

15. **Creative intelligence:** This is the reason behind their
    exploits. They always want an easy way out. They believe
    that necessity is the mother of invention. I am not the all-
    night prayers warrior type. I pray simple but active prayers
    because I understand what is needful – doing what will
    make the Angels come around me. Once I perceive the
    presence of the Order, being in the midst of the elemental
    entities of the Order, I would start speaking and in no time
    the results are seen around me. I also spend more of my
    time seeking wisdom, knowledge and understanding using
    my deep thinking gift. I had read in the Bible that the
    disciples needed not to pray and fast that much when Jesus
    is with them, until He is taken away from them. Later in
    the Bible Jesus said that the disciples would see Him, and
    again in John 14:18, He said that He would not leave
    them as orphans. Then in John 14:15-21, He said that it
    is possible for the Godhead to live inside someone. Then
    I saw from Genesis chapter 1:1 that Heaven was
    experiencing peace when Earth was in chaos because God
    was in heaven. Putting my facts together, I knew that if I
    can do the will of God then I didn't need long hours of
    praying for God's blessings and protection – 'touch not my
    Anointed' is the Lord's command. Those Anointed by
    God can analyze events in the Bible to enable them to live
    a perfect life – this is the gift of the anointing.

16. **Persuasive in nature:** All they are after is how to convince you of what they are saying and doing. That is what is in their heart. They already know the end; they are only working on you, to walk you into what they believe. So, any time you are with the Anointed, all they do is persuade you - using all their emotional gifts; smiles, tender eyes, tears in some cases, emotional complaints, sympathetic actions, compassionate attitude, articulating gestures, etc.

17. **Naturally seductive:** Apart from being emotional, they are also naturally seductive. It is difficult to deny the Anointed sexual advances. This is also a character of the devil, knowing that he was once in heaven. The angels that left heaven took wives without anyone questioning their abode. This is why they are also very good in business. They often use their instruments of expression - smiles and voice gimmicks - high and low tones in speech - to drive home their points. They appear to you with faces beaming like advertisements. Their clothes are eye-catching, with well-combined colours. They are sensitive to what you appreciate and they will use it to get your attention every time. You can see why those Anointed by the devil - who now works as the devil's agent - can lure anyone into its den, such that even Jesus

was afraid for the very elect. This is why we are in this discussion of wisdom, knowledge and understanding. Don't get me wrong, the devil too anoints people into his service.

Every burden shall be destroyed by the anointing (Isaiah 10:27). Whatever you desire is in the anointing. Get Anointed and you will definitely smile. My life is a living testimony of what God's arm can do. Moses gathered the elders of Israel together and God indeed Anointed them by taking from the spirit upon Moses so that even those in the camp did prophesy. The anointing is everywhere. Seek the anointing of the Lord and let's put the devil to shame as he sees your exploits. Don't accept anything less than success.

Alas! Your day to smile is here and I am very optimistic that you won't waste it – not now that you have received the Melchizedek Anointing through the deep reflective spiritual insight you have gained since you started reading this book. Remember, many are called, but few are chosen. What do the chosen few do? They achieve with the gifts of the Holy Spirit they receive. The Holy Spirit does the anointing and the anointing brings wisdom, knowledge, understanding and the power to execute God's will on earth. This book is to help us know what we need to do with the gifts in us, and how to best use the gifts for increase. Each of these gifts employed adequately is a rewardable service. Your exploits are what give God glory (Matthew 5:16). As Jesus went about doing good, His fame was announced all over the place. You don't keep your anointing in the morgue. No one lights a light and keeps it under a bushel. Set house on the mountain top. In fact Mathew 5 & 6 is a call to serve for exploits.

Before we leave this chapter let's see an abridged summary of the exhibited qualities of the Anointed:

- Prominent features – smile, happy, handsome, tender eye, etc.
- Self control in all things.
- Desire to live for and serve God.
- Respect for leadership – David's respect for Saul even when he hunted him, and Samuel's respect for Eli, are examples.
- Listening ear when in a discussion. An attribute they use to engage people's hearts to keep them talking and revealing secrets. This is why they are good at counselling.
- Attractive – charisma to attract people to themselves, and especially the opposite sex.
- Successful in all aspects of life.
- Easy to train in every aspect of knowledge, both mundane and ethereal.
- Talented in various walks of life, making them sought after.
- Servant heart - This is why many are highly employable.

They are most favoured employer's employees.

■ Academic intelligence and prowess – they are not known for failure.

In the following chapters, we will now dwell on the different areas in which the Anointed is called to serve. These are his exploits and where his/her reward will come from.

These qualities will now explain why the Anointed will do well in his/her chosen field of human endeavour and in his/her work in the vineyard as we shall see in subsequent discussion.

CHAPTER EIGHT

THE ANOINTED TEACHER

Jesus teaches while on Earth. The Holy Spirit is a teacher of reputation, with lots of experiences which He has gathered from the foundation of the Earth and He knows the heart of God because He proceeds from God. This is the primary duty of the Order – to teach whoever is willing to be taught. So the Anointed must possess this gift for him to be able to put together the pulsating codes he had received from the Order so as to better the lives of those living on Earth. This is why the Anointed lives in the Earthly Order, just as the functioning of a repeater station for a transmitting broadcast station.

Jesus says that what He does is exactly what He saw God doing. Teaching is a heavenly calling. Jesus taught daily at the temple after He had sanitized it by flogging and chased out those who mutilated it. This implies that we also have to repent and have a clean heart before we can receive the anointing teaching gift.

The repeater station only repeats the information sent out

by the base station. We have many of them, so that the atmosphere is infused with the same information, to subscribing customers. The teacher functions in like manner. The repeater station becomes the Earth Melchizedek Order, where the teacher operates from, and one would see that in certain seasons, if not always, pastors of various churches had taught the same wisdom without them formally agreeing to do that, but it happens as a coincidence. This is what is popularly known in Christendom as 'the oneness of the spirit.' The following facts are perceived of the Anointed teacher:

■ The Anointed is not just a teacher, but an established teacher, more than what the Jewish people call 'Rabbi', because whatever he/she does is done with the Anointing Order Character. He reveals whatever he hears from the Order. The disciples asked Jesus to teach them how to pray because they wanted to be like Jesus, who was going about doing good. He studies the Bible in order to teach it with deep revelations - 2 Timothy 3:16.

■ The teacher possesses the power of inquiry, because of the Anointing character in him. He asks deep questions as he learns. He sees what he teaches as solutions to problems. This was the character of Jesus, and it is the character of the Holy Spirit.

■ An Anointed teacher goes for the hard nuts and cracks them, searching through information banks and judging the present with the past, resulting in multitudes of wise sayings, wisdom, and parables. For instance the Anointed teacher may read Genesis 1:1-2 and start to ask the following questions:

1. Who created God?
2. Where is heaven?
3. How is it that only the earth was in chaos?
4. Why did He send the Holy Spirit?
5. Who is the Holy Spirit?
6. What is the purpose of the Holy Spirit?

The answers will come through the Holy Spirit: *The Spirit searches all things, even the deep things of God* – 1 Corinthians 3:11 (NIV). These secrets will send Him into a quiet state as espoused in Isaiah 30:15. All he/she wants to do is get answers to teach others. Anytime he/she is with you he/she will be asking these questions in order to have a clue in the deep secrets keeping this world alive- Deuteronomy 29:29, 1 Corinthians 2:7-8.

■ He uses illustrations or parables that have deep resounding meanings to send his messages across to his sea of admirers and drive home his/her point. He is good at using figures, pictures, video, etc, in teaching. He uses wise sayings and proverbs as he learns and teaches. These are all codes. The wise sayings just pop out at ease as he is teaching. His sayings are coded with important messages. We would also see that the success in the world today is the language of codes – mathematical equations, chemical equations, charts, laws, theories, etc. Jesus uses parables to teach messages that would have taken volumes of books, leaving you to make sense out of it. This is the beauty of the Holy Spirit helping us to speak in coded tongues. For instance let's see how Jesus explained what repentance and receiving the word of God is all about: *And no one pours new wine into old wineskins. If he does, the new wine will burst the skins, the wine will run out and the wineskins will be ruined. No, new wine must be poured into new wineskins. And no one after drinking old wine wants the new, for he says, 'The old is better.'* – Luke 5:37-39 (NIV).

- His/her classes are never boring because he/she possesses a sense of humour, making others laugh.

- He may be very aggressive in teaching to make you feel the importance of what he is teaching. He has a way of making you feel you have no choice but to do what he says if you must live. His words burn in your heart - Luke 24:32.

- He knows how to break down complex information to the audience he/she is teaching.

- Because the purpose of his/her teaching is problem solving he/she is not so concerned about theory but about physical applications and manifestations of what had been learned through the Holy Spirit. He is more interested in handy results – 'You say you are a Christian, then what? Where are the fruits?' That is how he reasons. His/her exam questions are difficult to answer because of his power of enquiry into problems. He/she expect to see 'thinking' presented on paper.

■ The Anointed teacher soon raises more teachers because he/she does not withhold information from eager learners. In effect he/she wants more people in the teaching profession so that the ideas he/she is teaching is sent across to more people.

What then is teaching? It is to impart knowledge of something or skill to others, which the Bible sees as the act of feeding the sheep. A teacher is one who teaches ideas and opinion, causing people to think and make a decision in response to what he says. People easily follow a teacher - John 1:35-39. If you can teach the word of God you will see multitudes clustering around you as the Bible says: *Many nations will come and say, 'Come, let us go up to the mountain of the Lord, to the house of the God of Jacob. He will teach us his ways, so that we may walk in his paths'* - Micah 4:2 (NIV).

Teaching exactly what the Order teaches will make life easier and the Holy Spirit will start revealing to you what to do so that you do not err. Many of us interpret the Bible wrongly because we do not have the Holy Spirit.

What then are benefits of teaching the word of God? We

can see this in Galatians 6:6-9: *Anyone who receives instruction in the word must share all good things with his instructor. Do not be deceived: God cannot be mocked. A man reaps what he sows. The one who sows to please his sinful nature, from that nature will reap destruction; the one who sows to please the Spirit, from the Spirit will reap eternal life. Let us not become weary in doing good, for at the proper time we will reap a harvest if we do not give up* (NIV).

Thus, as seen above, teaching can be of benefit in the following ways:

1. Physical reward from those you teach: e.g. in schools teachers receive salaries from the school fees we pay for our children. This implies that it is a profitable work of life.

2. If we sow the act of teaching in the lives of others, the Holy Spirit will teach us all the more so that we can teach more people. For instance, the books I have been able to write are a result of my teaching. Inspiration comes through your quest to teach. If you don't have the desire to teach others you won't receive inspiration from the Order.

3. A teacher yields to the Holy Spirit, because he is a learner himself and will ever reap the fruits of the presence of the Holy Spirit - even the devil reveals to those who learn from him in order to perpetuate evil. But our goal is to propagate good always, wherever we find ourselves. This

is why Jesus says: ... *learn from me, for I am gentle and humble in heart, and you will find rest for your souls* – Matthew 11:29(NIV).

4. A teacher does not give up - he hopes that some day his/her effort will be rewarded. This is why they are often told that their reward is in heaven. It is only a steadfast labourer who receives reward in heaven. This attribute is known by many, and that shows that the teacher is one with the heart of posterity.

The teaching task is a difficult one and could take you to hell because people do whatever their teacher tells them - Jesus says in Matthew 23:8, 10 that no one can be a teacher until the spirit of Christ lives inside of him/her, who will teach through such a one, using him/her as a vessel of honour, to disseminate instructions from the Order: *Nor are you to be called 'teacher,' for you have one Teacher, the Christ* (NIV). It is only when the spirit of Christ lives in a teacher that he/she can declare God in wisdom and might to the people he/she teaches - Galatians 4:6: *Because you are sons, God sent the Spirit of his Son into our hearts, the Spirit who calls out, 'Abba, Father.'*

Is it a job one should desire? Yes! It is risky but rewarding - James 3:1-9. Provided you do not teach outside Christ you won't lose your gains. Let everything you must teach have its root in Christ with a vision to putting things right, and He will pay you.

As we have seen in our discussions thus far, one of the qualities of the Anointed is the ability to teach others the knowledge inside him/her. A mother or father without the gift of teaching will definitely find it difficult to be able to bring up the children. The wisdom to live life to its fullest is in teaching. The cultures of the world have last until today because they were passed on through teaching.

The difference between the Anointed and the non-Anointed teacher:

- **Pride:** The Anointed teacher is concerned about how Christ will increase while he decreases, meaning that He talks more about Christ and not about worldly things. His examples are from the Bible. He uses Christ as role model. The worldly teacher takes people's heart from God but to themselves. This is why Jesus says of the non-Anointed teacher in Matthew 23:7: *They love to be greeted in the marketplaces and to have men call them 'Rabbi.'*

- **Focus on Jesus:** The Anointed teacher is like a compass which points everyone to the magnetic north - every magnet points to that pole. His heart is to make others look unto Jesus – Hebrews 12:2. This is where his/her value addition character and belief comes into play, because he/she sees the knowledge taught as a means of making the world a better place.

■ **Reward:** The unanointed teacher seeks reward from men, but the Anointed seeks his/her reward from God, asking and reminding Him for promotion and recognition, if he/she finds favour in His sight, not appearing to force God into rewarding Him, but making God to judge, wherever he/she functions as a teacher, knowing that God is righteous always.

■ **Equip:** He/she equips those he/she teaches with hard truths that will make them infallible to deceits, and that will make them able to succeed in life: *See, I have told you ahead of time. Heaven and earth will pass away, but my words will never pass away* – Matthew 24:25,35 (NIV).

■ **Enormous strength**: The Anointed teacher possesses more strength than the unanointed teacher, and this stamina is what encourages him/her to search through the banks of knowledge prayerfully.

CHAPTER NINE

THE ANOINTED PREACHER

In simple terms, preaching means to announce the good news to the world. This is what the Order is known for. Jesus says: *If anyone is ashamed of me and my words, the Son of Man will be ashamed of him when he comes in his glory and in the glory of the Father and of the holy angels* - Luke 9:26. We can see the Order personalities – Jesus, God the Father and the Holy Angels. These are they who will turn our situations around for good when we preach the word after being Anointed by the Holy Spirit. As I said earlier, the Holy oil anointing attracts the Holy Spirit because one has been consecrated for the work of God through the oil anointing. The Holy Spirit now comes to live inside the person, strengthening them to preach the gospel with all zeal. This is what brings grace and strength.

Knowing people, investing in them and retaining them remains the best way to success. This is why someone with a preaching anointing must understand psychology and be able to study people's character and behaviour as a feedback tool for his evangelical work. In the business world, what people value most is their customers. What God values most is souls. And we are here on earth to bring back the lost to Him. There are so many today that are lost and heading for destruction. This is why God told Abraham that he would become a blessing to the world.

Preaching is the act of soul winning which I see as the process through which the unsaved are added to the church daily, and they are retained for the great day when Jesus will return to judge the world. From the above definition, we can say that the act of soul wining involves identifying a soul, knowing the soul, identifying a church body that can help nurture the soul in line with the peculiar nature of the identified soul, encouraging the soul to undergo a training process which will help him/her mature in the spirit, encouraging the soul to desire the Holy Spirit, and then ensuring the soul has actually received Him. Not until the soul receives the Holy Spirit can he/she function as a sheep, and will therefore not abide till Christ comes.

The process outlined above is not going to be an easy one. This is why the Bible says the soul winner is wise. Why? It is because to win a soul, one has to apply wisdom, and wisdom can only come from God. So a successful soul winner is one who is already united to God through the Holy Spirit.

I would define preaching as the act of advocating a course

of action with a view to changing the mindset of people into behaving in favour of the message been publicly proclaimed.

The Anointed preacher preaches Christ and points them to Him. He/she may do this in the following manner to the people, explaining his/her message with a care of diligence, just as St. Paul started off with the, 'unknown God' caption. He could start off using the pattern below to drive home his point:

- **What a Love:** The Anointed preacher may start his/her soul-winning messages like this: 'When somebody shows us love by giving us gifts, we often try as much as possible to appreciate that kind gesture bestowed on us even if it will cost us something. Many young ladies have been lured into fornication because a man gave them a gift. In the same way many young men have slept with women of their mother's age because the woman could spend some money on them. If we are tempted to value material wealth to the extent that we can even trade our destiny, why can't we at least appreciate for once the unflinching love and care God has showed to us. In John 3:16, one could see the embodiment of the love God has accorded us: '*For God so loved the world, that he gave his only begotten Son, that whosoever believeth on him should not perish, but have eternal life*'. This is the most perfect gift the world has experienced since its creation - A gift that attracts God's attention into your life, the reason why we can now sigh a sign of relief from the torment of witches and wizards that placated our forefather's days. Freedom from oppression of traditional beliefs of killing of twins, released from the nest of witch doctors and all manner of evil doers. It is no secret to us here in Africa, and especially Nigeria, that there are evil occultist men and women who use human beings for sacrifices. These are what the name of Jesus Christ, the perfect gift from God has delivered us from.'

■ **The price for the gift:** He/she could start off with: 'If a witch doctor tells you to bring a goat, drink, food and money for sacrifice so that you will have eternal life, I am sure many of us will do anything to gain this life. Yet that promise from the witch doctor is false, because he has no life of his own to give. For you to have eternal life where your spirit will not be destroyed in the lake of fire called HELL you need to pay the following ransom.' He/she will then outline the price the people need to pay.

1.   **Believe that Jesus is your Lord and Saviour:** This is the cheapest price to pay in the entire world. Just believe as recorded in John 3:16 and that will settle it. You don't need to do it in a special place. Even while you are in your bathroom having a shower, you can just say 'Lord Jesus I believe you are my Lord and saviour'. That is all you need and you have a gift of everlasting life. This is when you actually confess your sins before God. As the Bible says: *He who conceals his sins does not prosper, but whoever confesses and renounces them finds mercy* - Proverbs 28:13(NIV)

2. **Confess Jesus before everybody:** The Anointed preacher continues – 'If you want to be saved from the turmoil of this world, a world where evil rules over righteousness, then you have to be closer to God and for you to be closer to Him you need to CONFESS His only son Jesus Christ before men. In Mathew 10:32: *'Everyone therefore who shall confess me before men, him will I also confess before my Father who is in heaven. But whosoever shall deny me before men, him will I also deny before my Father who is in heaven'*

You confess him when you preach the gospel as Jesus commanded in Mark 16:15: *'And he said unto them, Go ye into all the world, and preach the gospel to the whole creation'*

This is how it works; in the book of Revelation 12:10 the Bible recorded that Satan is all about accusing you before God: *'And I heard a great voice in heaven, saying, Now is come the salvation, and the power, and the kingdom of our God, and the authority of his Christ: for the ACCUSER of our brethren is cast down, who accuseth them before our God day and night'* (emphasis mine).

You cannot benefit from the Salvation, the Power, God's Kingdom and Jesus Christ's Authority if you do not confess him before men as your Lord and Saviour. The only way to avoid Satan's accusation is to confess Jesus Christ before men. You are either with Christ or with Satan.

3. **Be baptised:** When there is a death sentence upon someone, he will usually try all avenues, including appealing the case until he has exhausted all available avenue to avert the ruling of the court. For us Christians, the only weapon Satan has against us is our sin which he uses to accuse us before God. When you are baptized you will no longer be a slave under Satan. Your salvation starts from you confessing your sins to God, accepting and believing in Jesus Christ then getting baptized. See mark 16:16: *'He that believeth and is baptized shall be saved; but he that disbelieves shall be condemned'*

4. **Seek and Receive the Holy Spirit:** As he preaches and is now getting their attention, he opens up the crux of the matter – 'Before you can do this you must have confessed your sins, because the Holy Spirit does not dwell in filth'. This message will make those he is ministering confess their sins and repent for the onward possession by the Holy Spirit.

5. **Win souls for the kingdom of God:** Here the Anointed preacher will expand his message – 'The strength of any kingdom is in the number of people the King has in his kingdom and that determines to a large extent the strength of his army. What do you think God will do when he sees that the very reason He created the world has been wasted?

Do you think he will be happy to see that His enemy, the devil, have come to plunder His very home, a place he used to come down in fellowship with Adam? This is all the more reason why you have to depopulate the devil's kingdom by winning souls to God.'

A look at the structure above will inform everyone that the preacher knows what he/she is doing. This was why the multitudes couldn't resist John the Baptist and then Jesus as they preached to them.

Why is preaching important? Matthew 4:17-23 explains the beauty of preaching and teaching, and how they help each other. This is seen in the reason why Jesus had to preach in order to send the purpose of His birth across to His disciples as many began to hear Him and became healed of their ailments. So from Jesus' act in Matthew 4:7-23 we can see the following as the benefit of the gift of preaching, which the Order uses as means to get back the children of God into His kingdom.

1. Preaching is an instrument for mass publicity.
2. It draws the attention of others to you - Isaiah 52:7.
3. our feet will be beautiful, like those of a king.
4. A means to publish peace, publish good tidings - good news,

5. A means to decree things to past.
6. Someone with the anointing to preach can become:
7. Successful in evangelism.
8. A spokesperson as John the Baptist did, heralding the coming of Christ.
9. A secretary.
10. An event coordinator
11. A comedian.
12. A writer. *And it came to pass, when Moses had made an end of writing the words of this law in a book, until they were finished* – Deuteronomy 31:24
13. A newscaster.
14. A designer.
15. A company public relations officer.
16. A successful husband or wife.
17. A Successful teacher.
18. A Successful mother or father.
19. A Successful leader.
20. A successful planner because preaching is about strategies to succeed.
21. A successful musician.
22. A successful counsellor.

CHAPTER TEN

THE ANOINTED PROPHET

I will be starting this chapter with the revelation I had on the night of the 7th of July 2012. I saw myself going into the dark to pull out some people who were held bound. My wife and I decided to wait in a place which seemed to be a demarcation point between the light and dark. We waited, but no one came to join us and we decided to return. As we did so, we came across a church deceiving people using the inscription 'The Glory of God' on its entrance. But the front was dirty looking and I thought to myself that it was an occult gathering. The path to the dirty church was flooded with refuse and excreta everywhere. People were trooping in, until I came around and led the way out. However, as I led the way towards the light with my wife, her shoe got stuck and I had to help her out. As we delayed because of her shoe, other people saw us leading the way to the light, because they had thought there was no other way out and they all had to worship in the church. Many women trooped out and followed us out of the dungeon into a clear, beautiful path of light.

Other revelations the Order has revealed to me include the following:

- Strangers disappearing: This happened in a night vision I had some time in 2007. I was led into a town where strangers who entered the town were disappearing into a valley. As I got closer to the valley, I saw that these people were being devoured by monster-like creatures. Later in that dream, It was obvious that the natives were man-eaters. Connecting this to the monsters which devoured them in that valley paints one picture: the truth that those man-eaters were under the influence of the devil.

- Witchcraft in the church: Again in another night vision, a multitude of dwarfish creatures rushed into a church building. Then a monster in the form of a giant bird flew over the church trying to perch on the roof, but it could not. Also the multitude of those dwarf demons fled, seeing that the monstrous bird could not find a place to perch, and they proceeded into the compound of another church where they were harboured.

- Human beings tied to a mountain with chains: Another horrible sight that was revealed to me involved humans who were tied to a mountain which was under the care of a dwarfish woman. When I walked up to her she immediately dropped the keys to unlock the padlocks on my hands and the prisoners were let out of their shackles.

This is how the Anointed Prophet works. The Anointing Order opens His eyes to see the evil around him and what he needs to do to ensure that souls are delivered from the hands of the enemy. The Anointed Prophet makes things happen because the Order sends angels around him to put what he says into visible packets of instruction codes that have to be implemented by the Order through the angels. This is why scriptures tell us: Who is that that says a thing that the Lord has not revealed (Lamentation 3:37).

The gift of prophecy comes through an outpouring process just as the rains pours to the ground:

- Saul prophesied when he became Anointed and while he was looking for David; he and his servants also prophesied because the environment was charged with the prophetic gift.

- Seventy elders prophesied in the presence of God.

- Mary prophesied the moment the Holy Spirit lived in her.

- Hanna prophesied before the Lord in Shiloh.

The book of Joel 2:28 says: 'And it shall come to pass afterward, that I will pour out my spirit upon all flesh; and your sons and your daughters shall prophesy ...'

The Anointed prophet is more than just a prophet.

There are prophets and there are prophets. Jesus told us that
John the Baptist was more than a prophet: *And as they
departed, Jesus began to say unto the multitudes concerning John
…But what went ye out for to see? A prophet? yea, I say unto
you, and more than a prophet.* – Matthew 11:7,9. Reason being
that he cleared the path for the Messiah: *For this is he, of whom
it is written, Behold, I send my messenger before thy face, which
shall prepare thy way before thee.* – Matthew 11:10. If John the
Baptist is more than a prophet, then we are more than the
prophets of old because we have the Holy Spirit with us
always. We don't need to wait for Him to come upon us any
more. But He resides in us. Jesus confirms this when He says:
*Verily I say unto you, among them that are born of women there
hath not risen a greater than John the Baptist: notwithstanding he
that is least in the kingdom of heaven is greater than he.* – Matthew
11:11. The prophetic gift we receive is from the Order where
Christ belongs and so, the Order would not deny us
whatsoever we ask for in prayer. Prior to the coming of Christ
and the pouring of the spirit of God upon the earth and her
inhabitance, King David said: *his Lord said to my Lord* –
showing that it wasn't that easy to receive from the Order.
Moses had to know God through a burning bush. Elijah had
to go on a long journey to Mount Horeb. These days, God
would not allow us to suffer that long wait before He would

hearken to our voice. Jesus says that if our earthly parents know how to give their children good things, how much more our Father in heaven will honour the desires of those who diligently seek Him? God is raising Anointed prophets around you. Look ahead and you will see him.

The Anointed Prophet is a Praying Prophet.

The Anointed prophet thrives to live a righteous life. God said Abraham is a prophet and told him to walk before Him and be perfect. The power of prophecy is in the saying. That is where you know who is a prophet. God spoke to Abimelech in Genesis 20:7 that Abraham is a prophet and he shall pray for him. The spirit of God is behind the Anointed Prophet and he says exactly what the spirit says.

As I prepared this together, the Lord spoke to me that the year 2013 is a year for the consolidation of my increase. This is the promise of establishment. What this means is that the Lord is telling me now so that I can start to sow on time. As we entered 2012, the Order informed me that I would see increase during the year, but the increase would only come through mass publicity. This was how I went into book writing, knowing that God would certainly ask me what I had for Him to bless.

The Anointed prophet knows how to use physical creations to explain spiritual events. Let us see an instance in the Old Testament of how prophetic solutions were provided to restore sinners back to God until Christ came which now rendered the old practice null and void: *He is to lay both hands on the head of the live goat and confess over it all the wickedness and rebellion of the Israelites-all their sins-and put them on the goat's head. He shall send the goat away into the desert in the care of a man appointed for the task. The goat will carry on itself all their sins to a solitary place; and the man shall release it in the desert.* Leviticus 16: 21-22 (NIV). The Goat would bear the curses and sins of the sinner. Isn't that an elusive act, judging from the physical facts the verses express? But that was a prophetic solution that did work then. The reason it worked was because the Order had once done it in the Garden of Eden when God had to kill an animal to provide clothing for Adam and His wife. Have we ever asked how God did it? The understanding of that will be possible when we see how He created the elements of the world we see today. He only decreed and they happened. This is how the Order operates, and this action is carried out by prophets.

In the same way, the brazen serpent (Numbers 21:9), the Mantle of Elijah (2 Kings 2:11-14), the staff of Moses (Exodus 4:2-4) and Elisha's bow and arrows (2 Kings 13:15) all point to the fact that the Anointed Prophet decrees things into existence by simply linking the expected physical manifestation of his desires with existing objects created by the Order. Abraham had to look at the stars of heaven to enable him build his faith and to understand what God was preparing him for. In the days of Gideon, the Order used the dreams of the Medianites to explain to Gideon the outcome of the war he was about to fight. The Order's default character is a prophetic one. For instance, 'let there be', is a prophetic statement and the moment it was released, the Order backed it up with signs that were visible physically. This is why I decry the act of people claiming to be prayer warriors when they don't have the prophetic anointing.

We will be seeing how as an Anointed child of God how you can use the gift of Prophecy to beautify your life and that of others. From our discussion above we can comfortably say who is an Anointed prophet through the verses below:

Romans 1:19-20: 'Because that which may be known of God is manifest in them; for God has showed it unto them. *For the invisible things of him from the creation of the world are clearly seen, being understood by the things that are made,* even his eternal power and Godhead; so that they are without excuse:'

Isaiah 42:9: 'Behold, the former things are come to pass, and new things do I declare: before they spring forth I tell you of them.'

He hears a voice from God in order to guide his life and that of others - Isaiah 30:21. This is why many of them now use it as a means to extort money from people.

In the Order, prophets and ministers of the gospel belong to the sub-order of 'flaming fire' as espoused by David in Psalms 104:4. This is because they are always under the influence of the Holy Spirit, which sends a burning sensation into the hearts of those who hear the words the prophets speak – Luke 24:32. Jesus told us that the words He speaks are spirits and life. This is one easy way to know a prophet of God, who is Anointed into the Order of Melchizedek. Lamentations 3:37 says: 'who is he that saith, and it cometh to pass, when the Lord commandeth it not?'

The raising of an Anointed prophet and the fear of him
Why do people fear prophets so much? Let us simply say it is because they have eyes that can see your past and your future. They can tell you the sins you committed in the dark, which you thought that no one knew about. They can read your thoughts and still pretend they don't know when you are lying to them. They know the truth all the time, and because they value less about their lives, they can reveal your acts in public and make your repentance a mockery of sin. Especially for fake prophets who use the act for money making, they would want to reveal what they had seen about you in the company of others so that your positive confession will bring in more customers who they will deceive to release money from them. We must fear and respect them because of what they carry – the anointing of the Lord.

The book of Deuteronomy 18:18-22 says: 'I will raise them up a Prophet from among their brethren, like unto thee, and will put my words in his mouth; and he shall speak unto them all that I shall command him. And it shall come to pass, that whosoever will not hearken unto my words which he shall speak in my name, I will require it of him. But the prophet, which shall presume to speak a word in my name, which I have not commanded him to speak, or that shall speak in the name of other gods, even that prophet shall die.' This explains the fact that prophets of God are under the scrutiny of the eyes of God, hence He commanded that no harm should be done unto them. Even as He protects them so also He expects that they protect His secrets and only deliver them when instructed to do so.

God raises Anointed prophets from among you.
The presence of the spirit of Christ crying in the life of a prophet, as espoused in Galatians 4:6, is what makes him an Anointed prophet in the Order of Melchizedek. This is why I am not comfortable with people running from one prophet to another. And those who do this don't even know God yet. Looking through the life of Moses and other prophets of God you will see that they had a real knowledge of Him. A prophet of God works with the Spirit of God. So anyone claiming to be the prophet of God without the knowledge of Christ is a liar. The spirit of God doesn't lie. So no prophet of God would say a lie - John 16:13.

Primary responsibility of the Prophet

A prophet's primary assignment is to save a generation from the wrath of God. He has a heart of salvation and does not demand anything to do this. Any prophet who would demand money or gift from you is a criminal. Prophecies from God establish you without sorrow, because such prophecies carry His presence, leading to a joy of fulfillment.

Since 19th October 2008 when I answered this call, four years ago now, He has never abandoned me. My joy has increased daily. This is what the anointing of God does for you.

The difference between a prophet and a soothsayer

The devil has prophets too who he also speaks to and uses them to deceive people to cause them to err in the sight of God. The soothsayer tells you about things that will happen to you. The prophet talks of your relationship with God, and he has sound doctrine of God, teaching you what you need to do to avoid the wrath of God and be blessed by Him. The devil's own wisdom is but for a short time.

Key to prophetic utterance

A prophetic utterance is only possible and would bear fruit on the condition that who makes that utterance must be righteous before God: *The mouth of a righteous man is a well of life...-* Proverbs 10:11.

How to receive the gift

Our steadfastness in the house of God makes it possible to receive whichever gift we ask from God to enable us fulfill our duty and call. This is why Jesus called out: *But whosoever drinketh of the water that I shall give him shall never thirst; but the water that I shall give him shall be in him a well of water springing up into everlasting lif.* - John 4:14.

Prophetic instruments

Prophecy works with witness - Deuteronomy 31:28: '*Gather unto me all the elders of your tribes, and your officers, that I may speak these words in their ears, and call heaven and earth to record against them.*' This was Moses' farewell prophecy as he was near the day of his death. And indeed after his death, the Israelites did rebel against God. This is the kind of prophecy that God would take delight in, such that tell the people the truth about their relationship with Him.

A prophecy is something that is true and real. When you relate to elements of truth, your prophetic utterances will begin to bear fruit. This is why Jesus says to Pilate that those who hears Him hears the truth. And He made us to know that what God reveals to us is truth – John 17:17.

The following could serve as instruments of prophetic declarations as said earlier:

- Whatever is in your hand - Moses' staff., Elijah's mantle, etc.

- The creations of God, water, sun, moon, sky. You must have a perfect understanding of what they look like and how they function. These elements of creation have existed for ages and they can even bear witness.

- The testifiers of Jesus; Holy Spirit, water, blood of Jesus - 1 John 5:8.

- Whatever comes out of you - e.g. your sweat, finger nails, hair, bathwater, excreta, urine, spit, blood, voice, sneeze, etc.

Righteousness establishes your gift of prophecy so that you say things to pass - Job 22:28. If you have visited all manners of prophets, soothsayers, witches and doctors you need to come out of their seduction to become free. This is the reason many are suffering. Their souls have not been restored into the Kingdom of God yet.

How to know a fake prophet
Fake prophets do not possess sound doctrine. They can hardly lead people to Christ because they do not know Him either. Their prophetic sayings are filled with threats and such sayings and predictions, though may actually come to pass in some cases, makes the people fear the devil as these prophets lay

more emphasis on the influence and power of devilish shrines, witches and wizards, occult influence, etc. As they do so, they watch the response of their prey. The moment they are convinced that their prey is frightened as a result of their hypnotization, they will start making demands for money and other material sacrifices. In some cases, they fake miracles to ensure their prey is persuaded to release money into their coffers. They deceive their prey into unnecessary spiritual assignments. Their prey are seemingly those who have no knowledge of the acts of Jesus. They are those who want quick wealth and would refuse to hear the wisdom of God. Their hurrying nature is the underlying factor that makes them fall victim of these prophets. Fake prophets are only proud of signs and wonders as evidence of God working in them. They don't preach salvation and repentance which were the hall mark of Christ living on earth. - Mark 13:22-23.

The reason why fake prophets are deceiving the populace these days is simply because the world has gone after the winds, rebelling against every instruction of God and rather, would love to imbibe human wisdom. This is why the prophet Isaiah revealed the heart of God in Isaiah 30:8-10: *Now go, write it before them in a table, and note it in a book, that it may be for the time to come for ever and ever: That this is a rebellious people, lying children, children that will not hear the law of the Lord: Which say to the seers, See not; and to the prophets,*

Prophesy not unto us right things, speak unto us smooth things, prophesy deceits.

Looking at the statement above, we see that it is still a very relevant word from God to our generation. If we hear God through His Anointed prophets, the world will be the better for it.

Over time in our church, some members have come to meet me to say that my messages are not palatable to the ears as they centre on repentance. Some even told me that they would hire a pastor who would preach what they wanted to hear while I stay in the background as the church overseer! So we would say that the world is heading for destruction because we have rejected every instruction from the Order meant to lead us in the path of success that lasts as the blessings of the Lord brings riches and not sorrows.

CHAPTER ELEVEN

THE ANOINTED HEALING MINISTER

Why should the Anointed be a healing minister? We would answer this with what scripture says in Luke 4:18-19: 'The Spirit of the Lord is upon me, because he hath Anointed me to preach the gospel to the poor; he hath sent me to heal the brokenhearted, to preach deliverance to the captives, and recovering of sight to the blind, to set at liberty them that are bruised, To preach the acceptable year of the Lord.'

The Character of an Anointed Healing Minister
Let's take a look at the character of those in the medical profession - confidential, studious, compassionate, painstaking, a team worker, patient, listening to what the patient says, giving hope of survival, smiling, regretting every death as a result of not being able to proffer a cure, etc.

The zealous attitude displayed by the Anointed Healing Minister would best be explained by Matthew 11:12: *And from the days of John the Baptist until now the kingdom of heaven suffereth violence, and the violent take it by force.* The 'violent' referred to are those who know no fear. Prior to this time, people were held in bondage because they were sleeping while the evil one sowed tares in their lives. But the anointing is to preach the acceptable year of the Lord – a year of healing. This is the thought of God towards us. A healing minister knows that whatever is cursed will wither, so he curses every sickness and just watches it wither. He exhibits the character of Jesus and studies how Jesus healed all manner of diseases in the Bible. His favourite books of the Bible are the books of Luke and Acts. He also studies the acts of the prophets in the Bible especially Moses, Elijah and Elisha.

He does not take no for an answer. He will try out all possible avenues. He keeps on trusting God until he gets results.

How Healing Anointing works

■ Compassion

This is the default Character of the Anointing Order. This is why God provided the animal skin to clothe Adam and his wife. We would also see this compassionate character of the Order exhibited when Cain begged God to tamper mercy with justice and God had to give him a mark to ensure he was not murdered. Here is what Jesus also did: *And when the Lord saw her, he had compassion on her, and said unto her, Weep not.* – Luke 7:13

■ Command

The centurion in Luke 7:7-9 knows what command does. This is why those in the military who are used already to orders and what they are to achieve are dedicated ones when they become born again. The Anointed knows the authority he bears, and as such expects to see every ugly situation in his or others' lives bowing to his command. Jesus told the devil to get behind Him and it was so. Elisha commanded the River not to cause death and miscarriage, and the Bible says the land was healed and remained so. Now let's look at the centurion instance below:

Wherefore neither thought I myself worthy to come unto thee: but say in a word, and my servant shall be healed. For I also am a man set under authority, having under me soldiers, and I say unto one, Go, and he goeth; and to another, Come, and he cometh; and to my servant, Do this, and he doeth it. When Jesus heard these things, he marvelled at him, and turned him about, and said unto the people that followed him, I say unto you, I have not found so great faith, no, not in Israel. – Luke 7:7-9.

To the centurion, He knows that wherever Jesus is, Angels are there waiting to receive His command and act accordingly. And this was captured in Hebrews 12:22: 'But ye are come unto mount Zion, and unto the city of the living God, the heavenly Jerusalem, and to an innumerable company of angels.'

171

In another instance below we would also see how Jesus healed:

And he came and touched the bier: and they that bare him stood still. And he said, Young man, I say unto thee, Arise. And he that was dead sat up, and began to speak. And he delivered him to his mother. – Luke 7:14-15

'Let there be,' is the command of the Order. The sick man is transformed by the Order in a matter of seconds, once the word comes out of the Anointed. But before the Anointed says anything he usually waits for the Holy Spirit to speak. To ensure that his command yields fruit, he ensures that he is still a vessel of honour and can still hear what the spirit says. The Holy Spirit tells the Anointed what to say and the angels carry out the Order immediately. Since most illnesses are borne by the evil one who lives inside the patient, the presence of the Order around the sick is a sure hope of restoration as the demons will quickly pack their loads out of the life of the sick. This means that the command will only respond when the minister is still Anointed.

■ **Faith**

The Anointed thrives to please God always. The Bible says that without faith no one can please God – Hebrews 11:6. The faith he has in God is related to the trust in the anointing he bears. This is why the prophet Isaiah would exclaim: 'The Spirit of the Lord GOD is upon me, because the Lord has Anointed me' – Isaiah 61:1. He has great trust in the efficacy of the anointing he carries and whatsoever mantle or instrument of the anointing in him. This is why he is confident that whatever he says must surely come to pass. It is like someone who is confident of passing exams because he has studied the syllabus so well that he can explain the subject in question any time, any day. This is only possible to the extent to which the Anointed knows his God and understands His works –Daniel 11:32b: *'The people who know their God will be strong and carry out great exploits.'* And Hosea 6:3 says that we ought to pursue this knowledge of God: *'Let us know, Let us pursue the knowledge of the Lord. His going forth is established as the morning; He will come to us like the rain, like the latter and former rain to the earth.'* The Anointed hates suffering, as seen in Jesus' plea that the cup be taken over from Him, so he imbibes the advice in Hosea 4:6-7; 6:3, and seek after the knowledge of God in order to know Him – Jeremiah 31:34. Daniel revealed that...*even to the time of the end: many shall run to and fro, and knowledge shall be increased* – Daniel 12:4. The endtime church is the church which seeks after divine knowledge to be able to live in this world so as not to be engulfed in sinful knowledge and wisdom. Now that the

Anointed is filled with the knowledge of God, he would go ahead to decree healing and the results are there for all to see to the glory of God. Knowledge is embedded in wisdom. Now, wisdom is strengthened and beautified by seven pillars (Proverbs 9:1) – the seven spirits of God. The first spirit of God that comes into the Anointed is the spirit of the fear of Lord (Isaiah 11:2), and this is why scripture says that the fear of the Lord is the beginning of wisdom – Proverbs 9:10. How do we fear God? – Isaiah 50:10: *Who is among you that feareth the Lord, that obeyeth the voice of his servant, that walketh in darkness, and hath no light? let him trust in the name of the Lord, and stay upon his God.* What does this tell the Anointed? It makes him to know that those who must succeed in life must fear God and must not do anything outside the will of God else they would be in His bad books.

▪ Repentance

The Anointed healing minister knows that the prayer of a sinner is an abomination before God. He wants God to hear him when he prays, so he will seek avenues to make peace with those he has offended. He also seeks forgiveness even from those who have offended him. And because he watches the acts of Jesus as one who behold a movie scene before his eyes, his heart is filled with remorse. As he prepares for a healing crusade, all he does is plead with the Order so that his sins will not be counted against him until he gets a heartfelt assurance that his sins are indeed forgiven by God. Once the Anointed has repented, he goes ahead to tell those he would minister healing to do likewise so that God will see pure hearts, purged with hyssop. The Anointed healing minister's secret is contained in Matthew 5:8 – '*Blessed are the pure in heart: for they shall see God.*' Those who see God would definitely receive His touch and become healed.

■ Forgiveness

Jesus says that whichever sin the Anointed forgives is forgiven in heaven (John20:23). This is what gives the Anointed minister the boldness to forgive sins. Let's see an example: *Wherefore I say unto thee, Her sins, which are many, are forgiven; for she loved much: but to whom little is forgiven, the same loveth little. And he said unto her, Thy sins are forgiven.* – Luke 7:47-48. Anyone with a forgiven heart is a peace maker and peace makers are sons of God (Matthew 5:9). Every son of God is favoured by God, so the healing minister would not labour for the results of healing to show. No long prayers are needed. The only prayer would be the act of purging our hearts of filthiness. Our long stay in prayers without answers is occasioned by sins.

Anointed Healing Minister at work

■ The healing environment

Doctors operate in licensed hospitals where all the facilities and life support equipment are present. His nurses are well trained and they create the environment for him to operate. The healing minister ensures that he is operating in a Holy Ghost charged environment which brings in the presence of God. In that cloud of His presence, joy would certainly spring forth in the hearts of the people resulting in healing. But before the healing can commence, he ensures that he has equipped those working with him with knowledge about spiritual healing so that in one accord they will work. The choir must be purged with hyssop and their hearts must be pure enough to enable them see God in their praise and worship section. Everyone working with the Anointed must be sanctified and consecrated.

■ Good knowledge of the illness

Just as all medical professionals study illnesses, so the healing minister know much about various illnesses and their causes. We would see this in the book of Leviticus and how the Order proffered solutions to them. The minister does a lot of research and uses several case studies found in the Bible to build his faith. The writers of the books of the Bible usually describe all manner of illnesses that God visited on the earth because they had a perfect knowledge of them. Any minister undergoing a healing crusade without such knowledge will lack the spirit of thoughtful imagination, and that could hamper his ability to function in that calling.

■ Diagnostic tools

Just as the earthly medical doctor uses stethoscope and laboratory to work, so the minister uses the information from the Holy Spirit to diagnose the illness. This is how he knows what to do. In some cases Jesus forgave them their sins and in some cases he speaks a healing word. To some he taught them that healing is possible when the heavenly Melchizedek atmosphere exists. The Anointed healing minister must hear a voice and act on it accordingly. This is where in some cases the healing minister may want the sick person to confess or forgive someone, or plead for forgiveness from God or someone he/she must have offended.

CHAPTER TWELVE

THE ANOINTED IN BUSINESS

The Anointed is sound in economic principles. Though he may not be an accountant, he is surely one with a prudent heart. His workmanship shows in how he employs talents and gifts. His reliance on the fruits that wisdom yields makes him one with the heart of success. His heart yearns for increase, quality, reputation, and customer focus. These are the beauty of the gift of evangelism and heavenly race. This would be seen in St. Paul's admonition in 2 Timothy 4:7: 'I have fought the good fight, I have finished the race, I have kept the faith' (NIV).

He is a principled person, just as the character of the Order. Jesus displayed this over time as He relied on the instruction of the Order before He did anything. This is why the Anointed in business will never fail in his business ventures. He is aware that God had cursed the land in Genesis 3:17 and so whatsoever he is doing, in order for it to yield fruit he ensures that he has the approval and the blessings of God before going ahead to invest so that God would bless him.

Below are the principles he upholds to succeed in business:

1. **Principle of Increase:** The Anointed knows that the Lord says there will be increase for his chosen ones in various verses of the Bible. Deuteronomy 28:13 says that we shall be the head and not the tail. So the Anointed business man or woman, who has the Holy Spirit in him/her through the undiluted word of God, knows exactly that increase comes through God and would be ready to obey the laws and ideals posited by the Bible in relative terms. Proverbs 21:20 ESV: *Precious treasure and oil are in a wise man's dwelling, but a foolish man devours it.*

3. **Principle of bountiful sowing:** Sowing is investment. For instance, the prophet Jeremiah bought a field for the future in Jeremiah 32:6-9. The book of 2 Corinthians 9:6 says: *The point is this: whoever sows sparingly will also reap sparingly, and whoever sows bountifully will also reap bountifully* (ESV).

3. **Principle of saving:** This was what Joseph announced. Saving for tomorrow will enable you not to lack in the years of drought. This is what wisdom does to those that have it – Ecclesiastes 7:12. They understand the tide, and position their boat to sail ashore safely, no matter the storm.

4. **Principle of dedication:** The Bibles in Proverbs 6:6 says: *go to the ants you sluggard and consider its ways.* And the Anointed will actually go to see the ant at work to understand how it builds its anthill. He gets a piece of paper to document what he sees, and goes back to replicate it in his investment. Looking at how God dedicated time and resources to create this world would help anyone to do same. The Anointed in business shows good resource management skills – division of labour, resource sourcing, administration, customer focus, etc.

5. **Principle of thanksgiving:** Proverbs 3:9-10 says: 'Honour the Lord with your wealth and with the first fruits of all your produce; then your barns will be filled with plenty, and your vats will be bursting with wine' (ESV). The Anointed in business pays his tithes as due. He spends his money in evangelical missions. His heart desire is to see the propagation of the truth which the gospel offers. He is the heart of servants of God.

6. **Principle of Patience:** Jesus says in Luke 21:19: *In your patience possess ye your souls.* The Anointed is a patient explorer of his destiny. He turns in the facts in a stepwise order. He does not make a decision in a hurry and as such he is filled with the spirit of revival. Revivalists are patient people, who wait patiently to see their vision comes to pass.

7. **Principle of small beginnings:** Your beginning might be small, but your later end will be great if only you value little beginnings. Take a look at little children and watch them play. Gradually you will discover that they start making meaning out of what they are doing. As you watch more closely, you will see satisfaction in their hearts, which you will easily notice when someone scatters what they were playing with or stops them from playing – you will see tears in their eyes and sometimes they will report the incident to someone whom they feel should help them prevent you from shattering their investment. Children are very innovative. Though we don't take recognizance of their efforts, they have the heart to rebuild over and over again.

8. **Principle of lending:** He believes that he is a lender as the Bible says that we would lend to nations. He believes that he is only answerable to Jesus and would not want anything to affect that relationship. So instead of borrowing and becoming a slave, he starts with little beginnings. *Proverbs 22:7 ESV: The rich rules over the poor, and the borrower is the slave of the lender.* Romans 13:8 ESV *Owe no one anything, except to love each other, for the one who loves another has fulfilled the law.*

9. **Principle of mutual respect:** The Anointed uses the Bible to preach equality in business among his workforce,

and encourages them to be closer to Christ. Ephesians 6:5-9 ESV: *Slaves, obey your earthly masters with fear and trembling, with a sincere heart, as you would Christ, not by the way of eye-service, as people-pleasers, but as servants of Christ, doing the will of God from the heart, rendering service with a good will as to the Lord and not to man, knowing that whatever good anyone does, this he will receive back from the Lord, whether he is a slave or free. Masters, do the same to them, and stop your threatening, knowing that he who is both their Master and yours is in heaven, and that there is no partiality with him.* Colossians 4:1 ESV: *Masters, treat your slaves justly and fairly, knowing that you also have a Master in heaven.* He listens to the opinions of his workers and associates borrowing a leaf from what scripture says: Ephesians 5:21 ESV: *Submitting to one another out of reverence for Christ.*

10. **Effective resource management:** The Anointed uses the story of Gideon in Judges 7 to prune down unnecessary resources after hearing from God on what to do. This makes him to be able to recruit the right resource. Another story in the Bible that encourages and serves as wisdom for him is God's instruction concerning the usage of manna – the Israelites were not to waste it. He also gets insights on resource management from how Jesus selected His disciples – 12 out of the multitude that were about

Him daily, and then 70 for the evangelical work, until we have the 120 that were in the upper room.

11. **Investment guided by revelations:** From the story of Jeremiah, who bought a field in obedience to God, the Anointed goes ahead to inquire from God if he should go ahead or not in whichever business decision he is about to make so that he would not lost in that business venture: Ecclesiastes 5:13-14: *There is a grievous evil that I have seen under the sun: riches were kept by their owner to his hurt, and those riches were lost in a bad venture. And he is father of a son, but he has nothing in his hand* (ESV).

12. **Principle of investing for posterity:** He ensures that he leaves an inheritance for his children so that they will have time to serve God. King David did this for Solomon and if not for Solomon's wives that took his heart away from God, he indeed waxed great and judiciously used his father's assets to glorify God. The book of Proverbs 13:22 says: *A good man leaves an inheritance to his children's children, but the sinner's wealth is laid up for the righteous* (ESV).

13. **Guided by integrity:** Whereas he does business with tenacity, his heart is guided by the fear of the Lord. He is often taken aback by certain decisions which would compromise his faith in Christ. He hears a voice behind that tells him things aren't right the way he is going and

would make him withdraw. His watchword is Proverbs 11:3: *The integrity of the upright shall guide them.*

14. **Generous to the poor**: He imbibes the advice of God in the Bible, leaving behind whatever fell from his harvest for the poor: *And thou shalt not glean thy vineyard, neither shalt thou gather every grape of thy vineyard; thou shalt leave them for the poor and stranger: I am the Lord your God* – Leviticus 19:10. The Bible also admonishes us in Ecclesiastes 11:2: *Give a portion to seven, or even to eight, for you know not what disaster may happen on earth* (ESV). So the Anointed thinks of the welfare of the poor because the Lord has commanded that we do.

The difference between the Anointed and the ordinary man in Business is seen in the lies and cheating acts of the ordinary man, and overtime we would see that the venture would suffer stagnation because the breath of the Anointing Order is not in it.

CHAPTER THIRTEEN

THE ANOINTED IN ADMINISTRATION

An administrator is one who oversees and manages the affairs of government and other organisations - businesses, schools, hospitals, companies, churches etc. A wife with administrative capacity will definitely excel in marriage. I have decided to treat administration separately as an entity because of its relevance to the development of society, and the church. The Anointed uses his anointing to help plan and organize social events and meetings aimed towards evangelical drive. An administrative anointing helps one in financial planning and management, including office administration. Those with the administrative gift are always there to ensure that whatever work is put into their care in the church receives their productive attention, leading to fruitful results.

How does the Anointed use the anointing authority from the Order to become a result driven administrator? How does he put control measures in place to measure success? This will receive attention as we discuss further. But before we proceed, I want to differentiate between an administrator and a leader. While administrators are solely appointed based on their qualifications, a leader may emerge or be appointed. A leader thrives to undertake the risk of evolving processes that will make the administrator more efficient in carrying out outlined responsibilities and duties as it relates to his administrative power. While a leader with his quality may easily fit in as an administrator, it is more difficult for an administrator to become a leader.

Administration is segmental, while leadership is holistic in nature, involving a 'helicopter view' of what is needed to ensure the vision does not fail. A leader has a number of administrators working on specific elements of the vision he is driving.

This said, we now see the character of the Anointed administrator. Later in this book we will also talk about the Anointed Leader.

Character of the Anointed Administrator

We see this from the light of the Order. God is a leader. The angels administer His commands. Now with this we would look into the acts of angels, since our discussion aims to get the best in our administrative pursuit by explaining the advantages and encouraging every administrator to seek the anointing from the Anointing Order.

1. **Team worker** – The spirit of the Lord helps him to be motivated and respectful. Two angels were sent to destroy Sodom and they worked together to achieve that.

2. **Loyal to the leader** – The angels are loyal to God alone. One angel told John not to worship him because he was a fellow like him with the task of announcing Christ (Revelation 19:10, 22:9). They do not take glory for whatever they do, but receive their joy from the accomplishment of the work they do.

3. **Duty bound** – The angels are duty bound. They don't complain to God. What they know best is achieving set tasks and targets.

4. **Informed** – Angels are always around God and as such they are well informed. They know their job well and should not make mistakes in their decision. This is what earns them God's trust, as we see in Exodus 23:20.

5. **Focus** – Apart from being duty bound, they are focused and work like rays of light, walking in straight paths of righteousness.

6. **Organised** – The angels are organised, as we have seen above. The Order uses line of reporting to create orderliness – eg the counting of the children of Israel in the book of Numbers where the tribes have to camp round the tabernacle (Numbers 2). He has control over

the setting up of his team and would choose only qualified members as directed by the Holy Spirit, and not relying on deceitful CVs. Because of the presence of God in their midst the workforce yields its strength to deliver on promise rather than indulging in eye-service. This is also why God hates disorganized people.

7. **Detail Planner** – A look at the statement of the angel to Abraham about Sarah's fruitfulness would show how planning is the heartbeat of God. The pronouncement says 'by this time next year.' We have all read in the Bible of verses talking about seasons and time. A look at the plants and their fruitful seasons points to this fact also.

8. **Supervisory Executor** – This is the heart of administration. An Anointed administrator will leave no stone unturned in his tasks and targets. They execute and supervise so that there are no lapses either in quality or timely delivery. This is why at every creation, God inspects and gives His approval with a 'good' comment.

Difference between the Anointed and the ordinary administrator

The unanointed administrator is often so involved in a task, pursuing people to deliver, that he may become insensitive to the needs of others, making him/her act as a bully. Unlike the

Anointed administrator, he does not seem to show passion for detail and this shows in how he/she plans the job and the employment of resources, as these are often wasted. This would not be new, because the unanointed is seldom under the influence of the devil. The unanointed often takes responsibilities that may be poorly attended to, since he/she is often too distracted. They depend on their experience and would not give a thought to the wisdom of God. In no time they end up failing.

CHAPTER FOURTEEN

THE ANOINTED MUSIC MINISTER

I woke up on the morning of 2 of August 2012 with a song:

All around the world
I can hear the birds singing
All around the world
I can see the stars shining
All around the world
I can hear the sea singing
To the glory of your name

Fill me
With your glory this morning
Fill me
With your honour and power
Fill me
With your joy this morning
So I can shine like the stars in heaven

The song told me what my spirit yearned for and what God was about to do in my life, and that of the church. This is how to know an Anointed musical minister – he/she sings in the spirit. Severally in the book of Psalms we would see: *to the chief musician*, the leader or the Anointed Music Minister. The Anointed music minister sings only spirit-filled songs that send trills of emotions into the hearts of all present. All songs leads and points to Christ. He is guided by Psalms 150:1–6: *'Praise you the Lord. Praise God in his sanctuary: praise him in the firmament of his power. Praise him for his mighty acts: praise him according to his excellent greatness. Praise him with the sound of the trumpet: praise him with the psaltery and harp. Praise him with the timbrel and dance: praise him with stringed instruments and organs. Praise him upon the loud cymbals: praise him upon the high sounding cymbals. Let everything that has breath praise the Lord. Praise you the Lord.'*

The Anointed sings and plays musical instruments to praise the Lord's magnificence. The Bible tells of the extraordinary musical gift that was upon King David through the psalms he wrote and handed to the chief musician. He was intelligent and multitalented, radiating the essence of the Anointing that was upon him through music. The Levites were the singers and players of musical instruments in God's temple. We would see how the Bible referred to David's love for music in Ezra 3:10: *And when the builders laid the foundation of the temple of the Lord, they set the priests in their apparel with trumpets, and the Levites the sons of Asaph with cymbals, to praise the Lord, after the ordinance of David king of Israel..*

King David instituted music through writing and singing it and playing musical instruments. His playing of the harp sent the madness out of King Saul because the melody was filled with the Lord's anointing. Playing music could be said to be a major act of his life. The Bible made us to know in Psalms 89:20 that the Order Anointed David. The Psalms of David pointed to the glory of God and how music is loved by the Order. We are also made to know that Lucifer was chief musician in the Order before he left to form his own order here on earth which he now uses to seduce the world. The reason I have decided to talk about this character or gift of the Order is to enable us reap the reward that comes with ministering music in an acceptable manner on to God.

Society as we know it today boasts of variances of music and the influence of these music on society and church cannot be overemphasized. It is not uncommon to see young people and sometimes the old using iPods, Walkmans and even mobile phones to listen to music. There is also a variety of both electronic and acoustic musical instruments everywhere. The importance of music is also seen in the number of musical albums released daily into the market. Music has created jobs for producers, showbiz managers, CD duplication companies, musical instrument manufacturing firms, music software developers, etc. We have seen the formation of musical bands, and we see that those in the band share love and principles of working in teams, playing their parts with passion. During my recording experience in the studio, I have seen artists denying themselves sleep for days. Music even creates an opportunity to correct the ills in society, as many of these musicians are highly philosophical in their thoughts and the lyrics they compose. Music is a gift from the Melchizedek Order, which is why the Jews sang 'Hosanna' when they saw their King riding on a donkey into the temple.

People hum and move their bodies to any kind of beat. This leaves us with no other option but to ensure that people are guided appropriately to the right source of music and shown how humanity can reap the fruit music has to offer rather than exposing our generation to the drug addiction, sexual promiscuity and criminal vices that have taken people's hearts away from God.

The rhythmic movement of the human body to the sound of music, and the emotional flow that takes over our spirit when we listen to soft emotional songs, show that we were created with music in us. This will further explain what goes on in the Anointing Order. The hosanna song the disciples sang as Jesus entered into Jerusalem was so important to Him that when He was told to command them to keep quiet, Jesus replied that the stones would cry out instead, and this shows how God values worship songs.

We are going to look into the Bible and see how God instituted music in the Tabernacle, and from there we would see how the Anointed music minister functions in order to bring glory unto the name of the Lord.

Music in the Tabernacle

The tabernacle was made for service unto the Lord, and the Levites where to function in accordance to the instruction of God through Moses (Numbers 3:8). Scripture tells us that the setting up of the tabernacle was done with a specific layout, form, organisation and officiating responsibilities. The most captivating aspect of the service in the tabernacle was music - 1 Chronicles 9:32–33: '*And other of their brethren, of the sons of the Kohathites, were over the shewbread, to prepare it every sabbath. And these are the singers, chief of the fathers of the Levites, who remaining in the chambers were free: for they were employed in that work day and night.*' Day and night, they ministered in music before the Lord - day and night, did you see that? Another portion of the Bible that explained the place of music in the worship of God is 1 Chronicles 15:16: '*And David spake to the chief of the Levites to appoint their brethren to be the singers with instruments of music, psalteries and harps and cymbals, sounding, by lifting up the voice with joy.*' This is not a coincidence. God loves music that honours Him and testifies of His goodness to His children. The book of Amos 5:23-24, from which I would be explaining the character of the Anointed music minister, says: *Take thou away from me the noise of thy songs; for I will not hear the melody of thy viols. But let judgment run down as waters, and righteousness as a mighty stream.*

From here we see that the Anointed music minister would be one who would revere God, and God would accept his songs and the melody of his instruments because he is upright before God. So every music minister should endeavour to know God the more, through study of the scriptures and sound doctrinal maturity, so that he may minister God's word as a prophet to the nation.

Music in the Anointing Order

From what we have discussed, it is clear that God loves music. But before we may conclude on this, it is necessary for us to take a look at the book of Revelations, which actually explained the sight of heaven. Revelations 5:8–9 explains that music was in heaven: '*And when he had taken the book, the four beasts and four and twenty elders fell down before the Lamb, having every one of them harps, ... And they sung a new song, saying ...*' So we would see musical instruments accompanying the singing of the new song.

The Anointed Music Instrumentalist

Earlier in Revelation 4:1 John says: *After this I looked, and, behold, a door was opened in heaven: and the first voice which I heard was as it were of a trumpet talking with me...* This means that prophesies can be made through the playing of musical instruments. This explains that fact that the Anointed who plays musical instruments can prophesy the heart of God to the congregation: *Moreover David and the captains of the host separated to the service of the sons of Asaph, and of Heman, and of Jeduthun, who should prophesy with harps, with psalteries, and with cymbals: -* 1 Chronicles 25:1. A look into the content of most of the Psalms in the Bible will explain that the Lord can release prophecy through songs. Through the songs I compose and sing, I know what God is about to do in my life and how I am worshipping him in my spirit.

The Anointed Choir

What makes up the choir? The Anointed voices of many, with a song on their lips to honour and glorify God. Let us take a look at the number of the angels that make up the heavenly choir before the Lord: *'And they sung a new song, saying, Thou art worthy to take the book, and to open the seals thereof: for thou wast slain, and hast redeemed us to God by thy blood out of every kindred, and tongue, and people, and nation;*

and hast made us unto our God kings and priests: and we shall reign on the earth. And I beheld, and I heard the voice of many angels round about the throne and the…. and the elders: and the number of them was ten thousand times ten thousand, and thousands of thousands'- Revelations 5:9–11.

One hundred million angels singing in heaven in addition to the innumerable thousands of thousands! (Hebrews 12:22). Can you imagine that? This is the sound of joy in the third heaven and we need to imagine how they revere God by bowing down in His presence. This is what worship is all about. God expects this from us all the time, rather than all the prayers of complaints we often put forward before Him. If we would take the Lord's Prayer to heart (Matthew 6:10-13), then God is expecting us to replicate this here on earth: *Thy kingdom come, Thy will be done in earth, as it is in heaven.* This must happen before we start to pray for His favour and forgiveness, preserving us from temptation and deliverance: *Give us this day our daily bread. And forgive us our debts, as we forgive our debtors. And lead us not into temptation, but deliver us from evil:* Because we have honoured Him knowing that His kingdom is filled with power, honour and glory: *For thine is the kingdom, and the power, and the glory, forever.* So our choir should replicate these values in heaven, in holiness and sanctity, on earth. Only then will we experience the mighty movement of God in our midst. The learning of spiritual songs, psalms and hymns is possible when we are redeemed. Revelations 14:3 says that only the redeemed could learn the songs angels sang in heaven. How could we ever sing to bless God when we cannot understand what angels sing in heaven to honour Him?

From what we have discussed so far, we would see that the Anointed music minister is one filled with the joy of the Lord in his/her heart. His/her ministration brings down the presence of the Lord. He/she must have a repenting and forgiving heart, dedicated to the service of the Lord in His altar.

CHAPTER FIFTEEN

THE ANOINTED IN SPIRITUAL WARFARE

In both government and public establishments, you notice that the higher you climb the ladder of authority, the calmer the office environment becomes, until you get to the topmost position where the power of influence lies. This is what wisdom does to anyone who has it – it brings calmness and confidence (Isaiah 30:15). Anyone claiming to have power who shouts at the threat of an opponent is powerless. When the Jewish authorities brought the woman caught in the very act to Jesus, His calm nature sent waves of authority across to them until He passed that judgment that freed her. Those in authority are only strategists and do not tremble at every glimpse of satanic overture they perceive.

Before we continue with this discussion, it is necessary for us to know what spiritual warfare is all about. The Bible says we should be as wise as the serpent and as harmless as a dove – Matthew 10:16: *Behold, I send you out as sheep in the midst of wolves; so be wise as serpents and harmless as doves.* Spiritual warfare is not about killing our enemies with Holy Ghost fire, but by, through wisdom, building a society where love and unity may thrive. The serpent withdraws from public scrutiny, not drawing attention to itself, yet battle-ready. While we would be battle ready at all times like the serpent, we are advised to be harmless. Isn't this surprising? The popular verse often quoted in Ephesians 6:12: *For we wrestle not against flesh and blood, but against principalities, against powers, against the rulers of the darkness of this world, against spiritual wickedness in high places.* To be able to understand this, as it is not a right thing to judge scripture messages through a singular verse and seeing it as self sustaining, we should take a look at Revelations 13:18: *Here is wisdom. Let him that hath understanding count the number of the beast: for it is the number of a man…* meaning that the mark of the beast may just be economic policies that will make one to denounce God or do the things that God hates just as Solomon worshipped the gods of his wives. Now looking at Ephesians 6:12 again, we would list out the following:

■ We do not fight against flesh and blood, hence spiritual warfare is about having a knowledge of the spiritual: *Which things also we speak, not in the words which man's wisdom teacheth, but which the Holy Ghost teacheth; comparing spiritual things with spiritual* – 1 Corinthians 2:13. This will enable him/her to judge rightly.

■ We wrestle against the powers that be which make laws and policies and enforce them. These powers rule this world with the authority they receive from the devil, which makes them wicked, and the righteousness of God is not in them. This implies further that these kings, queens, governors, presidents, managing directors, grand masters of occult groups, even false pastors, will ensure that those they oversee are led out of the path of righteousness by feeding them with false wisdom as a result of the spirit of the devil in them. How do we get out of these? The Bible tells the Anointed what to do: '*Wherefore take unto you the whole armour of God, that ye may be able to withstand in the evil day, and having done all, to stand. Stand therefore, having your loins girt about with truth, and having on the breastplate of righteousness; And your feet shod with the preparation of the gospel of peace; Above all, taking the shield of faith, wherewith ye shall be able to quench all the fiery darts of the wicked. And take the helmet of salvation, and the sword of the Spirit, which is the word of God: Praying always with all prayer and supplication in the Spirit, and watching thereunto with all perseverance and supplication for all saints.*' - Ephesians 6: 13-18. From here the Anointed would extract the following:

■ He puts on the armour of God. This is the knowledge of God which will enable him to discern spiritual environments and take precautionary measures. This action is what the Bible termed as fleeing from every appearance of evil (1 Thessalonians 5:22). His quest for knowledge makes him closer to God through the observance of the command of Jesus Christ, so that over time he becomes filled with the fullness of God's Holy Spirit and becomes one with the authority of power and the wisdom of God. Thus making the spirit of Christ to cry in his heart, leading to his heart being filled with understanding so that his mouth shall speak wisdom always. Once this has taken place in his life, he need not be afraid of the antics of the devil and those spiritual warfare prayers of many so-called believers which they do with much shouting for fear of being intimidated by the devil, will give way to the preaching of the gospel with much boldness as a result of being filled with the Holy Spirit.

■ Now that the Holy Spirit has taken His place, bringing to remembrance the words of the Order in the Anointed, those words in the Bible he had earlier read and studied, he is led through the path of righteousness as the word of God shines as a lamp upon his feet daily, and that takes him farther away from sin. His spiritual warfare prayers will gradually give way to prayers of praise and adoration unto God. Now he no longer lives in fear. Many argued that the disciples did pray loudly on that day of Pentecost. Of course they did, but we should not forget that these disciples were living in fear in that crowded inn. They were in that room as sheep without a shepherd and the thought of the wolf coming was the fear that lived in them until the Holy Ghost came. Even at that, was it all that received the Holy Ghost that succeeded in spreading the gospel with outstanding results? It was those who had learned the truth and who could compare scripture verses. We grow maturely daily through the receipt of spiritual illumination in the word of God. Those who have peace in their spirit do not groan, and as long as you do not groan in your spirit you won't make a noise in your prayers. I prefer heartfelt meditation and communing with God. I prefer God to rebuke me of the sins I have committed so that I would plead for forgiveness and repent so that my actions will win souls to Him.

■ Based on his knowledge of God, he now engages in prayers and supplications, entreating the Lord to accept the meditation of his heart: *Let the words of my mouth and the meditation of my heart Be acceptable in Your sight, O Lord, my rock and my Redeemer* – Psalm 19:14. The maturity of the Anointed is seen in how he communicates with God. You don't see elements of fear and emptiness in his prayers. He talks the heart of God all the time.

To this end we would see that spiritual warfare is about knowledge, understanding and wisdom. This is because the devil's easiest way to get you into his net is by feeding your mind with information leading to thoughts that will eventually envelop you which will show in what you desire. Someone who wants to be free from warfare would not desire what the heathen goes after – jewels, electronic gadgets, fashion, money, etc. As long as we go after these, all we need is wisdom from God on how to live with these realities. The seeking of such wisdom is the reason we would study the Bible, meditate on the words we have read into our spirit, and live by them. If we obey God we won't need to offer all those noisy all-night prayers as someone who have being defeated in the war front.

Let us see what warfare looks like from the following Bible verses:

■ The fall of man: *Now the serpent was more subtil than any beast of the field which the Lord God had made. And he said unto the woman, Yea, hath God said, Ye shall not eat of every tree of the garden? And the woman said unto the serpent, We may eat of the fruit of the trees of the garden:* - Genesis 3:1-2. The fact that Adam did not make reference to the serpent shows that he didn't see him: *And the man said, The woman whom thou gavest to be with me, she gave me of the tree, and I did eat* – Genesis 3:12. He saw only his wife there or he might have decided not to recognize the devil's presence, which could mean that the serpent was working on the thoughts of Eve, from where she was manipulated. So while we are shouting in prayers, what happens to the information we send into our minds daily? Have we fled from all appearances of evil? If we can't flee anymore because the devil has placated our surroundings with devilish subtle information wherever the head would turn, then we need divine wisdom from God to live a sinless life. As long as we don't owe the devil anything, he won't come after us. We would only have the angels to minister unto us – Matthew 4:11

■ The withholding of Daniel's prayer answer – Daniel 10:12-13: *Then said he unto me, Fear not, Daniel: for from the first day that thou didst set thine heart to understand, and to chasten thyself before thy God, thy words were heard, and I am come for thy words. But the prince of the kingdom of Persia withstood me one and twenty days: but, lo, Michael, one of the chief princes, came to help me; and I remained there with the kings of Persia.*

■ The Temptation of Jesus: *And when the tempter came to him, he said, If thou be the Son of God, command that these stones be made bread. But he answered and said, It is written, Man shall not live by bread alone, but by every word that proceedeth out of the mouth of God. Then the devil taketh him up into the holy city, and setteth him on a pinnacle of the temple, And saith unto him, If thou be the Son of God, cast thyself down: for it is written, He shall give his angels charge concerning thee: and in their hands they shall bear thee up, lest at any time thou dash thy foot against a stone. Jesus said unto him, It is written again,*

Thou shalt not tempt the Lord thy God. Again, the devil taketh him up into an exceeding high mountain, and sheweth him all the kingdoms of the world, and the glory of them; And saith unto him, All these things will I give thee, if thou wilt fall down and worship me. Then saith Jesus unto him, Get thee hence, Satan: for it is written, Thou shalt worship the Lord thy God, and him only shalt thou serve – Matthew 4:3-10.

■ What do these passages tell us? Simply put, they tell us that spiritual warfare is about information dissemination. It is more about a battle of the mind. So the devil's antics are aimed at manipulating our minds and making us feel that our salvation is fake and would not deliver us. And whoever disseminates information must understand the authority behind the information being disseminated. This is why even the devil disseminates information contained in the verses of the Bible, tainting them with his motives of destruction, knowing that God's words are powerful. Shouting prayers only points to our feeling of powerlessness. Jesus says that all power belongs to Him, if truly Christ lives in us, where is His power working in our lives if we have to shout in our prayers as though we are orphans? King David advised: *Tell it not in Gath, proclaim it not in the streets of Ashkelon, lest the daughters of the Philistines be glad, lest the daughters of the uncircumcised rejoice* – 2 Samuel 1:20. Even prophet Micah advised same: *Declare ye it not at Gath, weep ye not at all* – Micah 1:10. How will unbelievers see us when all we do is shout prayers as if our God is deaf? They will not repent. Who wants to serve a deaf God anyway? We must show some level of decency and decorum in our prayers. The only way out is by understanding every word in the Bible and the reason why they were spoken by God.

The devil knows that many believers will eventually shout, casting and binding in their prayers, which usually shows a frightened state of mind, so all he does is fill the environment with offensive and foul information so as to provoke us into anger. What have I done? I have decided not to give such information a second thought, thereby making them passive in my thoughts. As long as they are passive, I will never remember them. It is what we remember that influences the kind of lives we live.

In my book 'Battles beyond the Physical,' I explained that the sin path is made up of four elements: Perception, Thought, Communication and Action. Once any of these four elements is knocked out, there will be no sin. I have seen that the occult, witchcraft, witch doctors and their like, don't make a noise in their requests to the devil because they know what the devil can do. One would hardly know they are even in a meeting, yet they have turned this world into an evil paradise through persistent meetings with the devil in the night, in their gathering and carrying out his instructions. A look at organizations worldwide would also prove the point that good decision-making strives in an environment of quietness and confidence (Isaiah 30:15). All institutions of learning, including the universities, are as serene as the grave, and we would judge that great minds have been developed in these institutions over time. A spiritual prayer warrior is not one who prays volumes of words, but one who meditates on the word of God and uses them to plead a course before God, decreeing things and seeing them established. I see prayer for specific need as a project with start and finish date. So if we keep on repeating the same lines of prayers without results, we should consider our ways before the Lord. God is not deaf. This is why Jesus says that we must be as wise as the serpent. So instead of shouting our prayers all night, I would advise that we gather more to learn about Jesus Christ, His actions and commands, and follow suit. This way, believers won't be seen as arrogant people who are out to fight the neighbours they are supposed to love and be at peace with.

The following is the wisdom which guides the Anointed in spiritual warfare:

1. **Seeking peace:** Christ has given us peace – John 14:27. Those who have peace don't live a life of fear and their prayers will be filled with statements of love. The scripture says that we should be at peace with all men.

This can only come through negotiation leading to agreement (Hebrews 12:14,18, Matthew 5:25, Amos 3:3) or through separation and fleeing, because light and darkness cannot come together. Once we all have a common salvation (Jude 1:3-7), we may live in a peaceful and loving environment. Even in the midst of our rebellion, God says He is ready to reason with us so that peace would reign (Isaiah 1:18), and at the end of that reasoning He sent Jesus to teach us His ways and as a sacrifice for our sins. The enemies we have and contend with today as Christians is our inability to live as Christ commanded. For instance see what He advises: *If someone strikes you on the right cheek, turn to him the other also... -* Matthew 5:39. In that same chapter of Matthew in verse 9, Jesus says: *Blessed are the peacemakers: for they shall be called the children of God.* The tones of our warfare prayers shows that we haven't imbibed the advice of Jesus yet. Many believers are too proud to beg for forgiveness from their neighbours. Many unbelievers have refused to repent because they have seen that many believers only claim to love God when all is rosy around them, and therefore their service to God is born out of selfish intent. Imagine a believer whose preaching is only centred on the testimony of the miracles and blessings he/she had received, without teaching others the word of wisdom which Christ lived with. Many are in need of wisdom and if we would teach it to them, they will follow us down to church. Peace of mind comes when we trust in God (Isaiah 26:3). And this boils down to the fact that many of those who engage in spiritual warfare prayers are those who fear the devil because they don't have the full knowledge of God which will make them trust in Him totally in their heart.

2. **Favour from God and his neighbours:** We have a word of understanding from Luke 2:52: 'And Jesus increased in wisdom and stature, and in favour with God and man.' The Anointed knows his God because he hears what God says, and that makes him strong in every aspect of his life. As long as people will depend on your wisdom to live, as you continually let them see the God in your life when you teach them and reveal divine secrets to them, you will have favour from your neighbours. I have experienced more regard from people, especially unbelievers. My greatest problem has been those who claimed to know God. They are the ones who will challenge every oracle from God, and will time after time engage in long warfare prayers as if their God was dead, and resort to praying in a mourning mood like someone who has lost a close relative. The centurion's servant was healed because of his faith, but I have seen over time that

many so-called Christians do not know their God, hence the fright they have, which is easily seen in their warfare prayer points. To me prayers are for direction, and direction comes through wisdom. The Lord spoke to me some time in 2011 to say that the only way to overcome trials is to have the right wisdom. With the wisdom of God, we would be able to overcome the pressures of life we experience, which have also resulted in the long list of prayer requests Christians carry about from one church to the other.

3. **Seeking unity:** The Anointed seeks unity among brethren with the word of truth. Scripture tells us that the apostles achieved because they were united at the beginning. A time came also when they started disagreeing, as seen between Peter and Paul. Even during Jesus' days, James and John had brought in their mother to negotiate their position with Christ. And St. Paul had to settle the disagreement that was in their midst, in 1 Corinthians 1:12: *Some of you are saying, 'I am a follower of Paul.' Others are saying, 'I follow Apollo,' or 'I follow Peter,' or 'I follow only Christ.' ... of you is saying, 'I belong to Paul,' or 'I belong to Apollos,' or 'I belong to Cephas,' or 'I belong to the Messiah.'* What is the cause of this division if our vision is Christ? Materialism, seeking fame, money, politics in the church, etc. Today the Christian body worldwide is divided. The Pentecostal church believed

they were the ones who were filled with the Holy Spirit and as such they would be the ones to make heaven. Other denominations claim the same. But my take is, since I am called into a commission, I would only act as God says, and that saves me from being a part of the growing division in the Christian body today. A united entity is a strong entity. If so, our long nights of warfare prayers would be turned into nights of praise and adoration to our Lord.

4. **Respect for hierarchy:** One of the problems we have in Christendom is lack of respect for the spiritual authorities in our midst. I have seen that most people who engage in long prayers of warfare are arrogant people and many hardly know the constitution of the nation they live in. Some do not even vote or contest in elections into offices of authority. How then can the righteous rule so that the people will rejoice? When the wicked assume power, they will be the ones to stay all night in their churches shouting 'Holy Ghost fire' – casting and binding. Where were they when elections were being conducted? What have they done with the knowledge of God they have acquired? Spiritual warfare is about knowledge and the rightful application of it, not necessarily nights of prayers of fright. There are hierarchies in heaven – we have angels and archangels. Christians should also learn to respect authorities in the church and society.

5. **Doctrinal maturity:** The book of Titus 2:1 says: *But speak thou the things which become sound doctrine.* Immaturity in matters of God is often the reason many believers shout in their prayers as though they are being tormented by evil spirits. They even complain more than those they see as their unbelieving folks. They would take a verse of the Bible and off they go, casting and binding. Most disagreements that would have been settled through dialogue and understanding are postponed till midnight, when they would start to cast and bind. Many even spend their productive hours bemoaning their fate. All these are the result of doctrinal immaturity. Once we are matured in the things of the spirit, our carnal attitudes may give way to love, which will now reside in our hearts as we see everyone as the image and likeness of God.

6. **In control:** Most of our all-night prayer points show that believers have lost control of the world Christ handed over to them because of poor doctrinal knowledge, as earlier discussed. Was Jesus hiding from those in authority who use their power to oppress the people? Let's find out: *And it came to pass, that after three days they found him in the temple, sitting in the midst of the doctors, both hearing them, and asking them questions. And all that heard him were astonished at his understanding and answers* – Luke 2:46-47. He sat in their midst to teach them and answering

questions. What do we do in our case? We gather all night, praying and shouting, waiting for God to fight them, while we continue in sin. And again we would see what He did at the temple: *And he went into the temple, and began to cast out them that sold therein, and them that bought; Saying unto them, It is written, My house is the house of prayer: but ye have made it a den of thieves. And he taught daily in the temple.* The house of God is the house of prayers for repentance. But the reason people commit sin daily was lack of knowledge about God, and so Jesus sat there daily to teach them and open their understanding. Warfare prayers were not needed in Eden. It was the fall of man that resulted in warfare prayers. If we would live in Christ Jesus, we would not have need of them. Jesus only instructed the devil with the word that was written, and would not fall for the devil's tricks.

7. **Who owns the battle?** Titus 2:9 says the Lord is the only one who can rebuke the devil. We are also made to understand that those who overcame the devil with the blood of the lamb and the testimony of their mouth were the angels (Revelations 12:7-11). The book of Daniel 110:13 told us that it was only Archangel Michael who could defeat the devil. This is wisdom. All we need to do is to ensure we do not offend the angels, by continually confessing Jesus wherever we go after studying and getting

the approval of God to teach His word (2 Timothy 2:15). This is what I understand as spiritual warfare – feeding people with knowledge and understanding so that they have the power and wisdom of God, because they now know Him as a means of active defence against the antics of the devil. The Israelites cried to God in their prayers because they didn't have a perfect understanding of who He is. Even in the wilderness the Ten Commandments which were supposed to lead them into understanding God were not adhered to. The Anointed only seek to know God more and to do His command. This way, the Lord will be there for Him with a decree: *Touch not my Anointed, and do my prophets no harm* – 1 Chronicles 16:22. The Bible says: *the Lord knows how to save those who serve Him from troubles* – 2 Peter 2:9. Our long prayers of shouting in fright of the enemy are as a result of our sins and disobedience to His instructions. But if we would repent and do His command, and avoid sin, we would have less warfare prayer requests. We have more wickedness in society today. which is making it difficult for us to please God. For instance, we know that the Bible says in Proverbs 11:26: *People curse those who hoard their grain, but they bless the one who sells in time of need.* Yet we still have people who hoard food, fuel, and other substances needed by the people to live during the time of scarcity, and later such people engage in all-night prayers to God. A cursed person is cursed and should repent and not go back to his/her own vomit.

While I am not against warfare prayers, I am against long, loud all-night prayers which only tell the enemy that we don't know our God. Daniel prayed secretly, alone. The Bible says: *'The effectual fervent prayer of a righteous man availeth much'* - James 5:16. Another passage says: *'Righteousness exalts a nation, but sin is a reproach to any people'* - Proverbs 14: 34. Even when Nebuchadnezzar condemned Shadrach, Meshach and Abednego to death by fire, there was no place where they cried out to the Lord, but their righteousness delivered them. And here is the testimonial of their righteousness from the mouth of an unbelieving King: *Then Nebuchadnezzar came near to the mouth of the burning fiery furnace, and spake, and said, Shadrach, Meshach, and Abednego, ye servants of the most high God, come forth, and come hither. Then Shadrach, Meshach, and Abednego, came forth of the midst of the fire* – Daniel 3:26.

Why is it that our righteousness is not speaking for us? What has happened to our faith? The answer is easily seen in our prayer requests and the utterances from our hearts during over-popularized all-night prayer meetings. I would encourage Christians to seek righteousness instead of offering long prayers of fright, binding and casting, seeking deliverance when they have not repented. Many of us today have decided to act like Philip who sought to see God when he was not through with the commands of Jesus yet, which points to the heart of God: *Philip saith unto him, Lord, shew us the Father, and it sufficeth us. Jesus saith unto him, Have I been so long time with you, and yet hast thou not known me, Philip? he that hath seen me hath seen the Father; and how sayest thou then, Shew us the Father? Believest thou not that I am in the Father, and the Father in me? the words that I speak unto you I speak not of myself: but the Father that dwelleth in me, he doeth the works. Believe me that I am in the Father, and the Father in me: or else believe me for the very works' sake. Verily, verily, I say unto you, He that believeth on me, the works that I do shall he do also; and greater works than these shall he do; because I go unto my Father. And whatsoever ye shall ask in my name, that will I do, that the Father may be glorified in the Son* – John 14:8-13.

God has raised pastors for us, who will lead us to Him because they hear His voice and what He wants His children to do for Him. When a servant of God faces the congregation to minister unto them, God releases an oracle which includes His command. But over time, the problem with the church is that they don't want instruction from God, all they want is an outright answer as if God is a casino machine so that they would throw in some coins in the form of prayers and God will roll out jackpots for them as blessings.

Now let us see what Jesus says further in John 14:14-15: *If*

217

ye shall ask any thing in my name, I will do it. If ye love me, keep my commandments. Answers to our prayers are tied to our observance of His command. So instead of shouting in our prayers as if having a war with God, we should repent from all evil manipulations in our hearts and heed His advice to keep His commandments to live in peace and love, and in unity of fellowship with God. My God is not deaf and He is not dead either.

CHAPTER SIXTEEN

THE ANOINTED INVENTOR

It is my sincere belief that every inventor of repute who adds value to society bears a mark from the Order which enables the Order to communicate with him wherever he is, so as to bring to pass the Order's expectations of him. This is why I believe that God warned that no one should touch His Anointed. Who is God's Anointed if not the one bearing His purpose in heart? And what anoints them if not the oil of joy? So the anointing oil is the physical mark of recognition for someone the Order had chosen from the womb to be a solution provider and a leader of conscience. Jacob was chosen from the womb. Jeremiah was chosen from the womb, and so, also, were Samson, John the Baptist, King David, etc.

Let us also see why Cain's descendants were the first recorded inventors in the Bible - Genesis 4:20-22. Cain's birth as the firstborn automatically made him one chosen by God as confirmed by the Bible (Exodus 13:2). Let us also not forget that Cain heard God and experienced His presence as confirmed by Cain's conversation with God - Genesis 4:9, 14. If it had not been for satan possessing him to do evil by killing his own brother, Cain would have been much more successful than he was. He was marked by the Order on his face after he pleaded with God, which I would liken to the anointing which prevented anyone who saw him from killing him, judging from God's command not to touch His Anointed - 1 Chronicles 16:22.

Cain's descendants were the first inventors, as the Bible recorded, which I also believe became possible because Cain had been earmarked by God with a mark on his face, which made it possible for the Order to follow him about. That would automatically mean that the Order also followed his descendants because they also inherited the mark upon Cain. It won't be out of place to conclude that the mark upon Cain which is a seal of recognition from the Order is what would explain why Cain himself could build a city, the first to do such, recorded in the Bible - Genesis 4:17.

Many use their gift of invention for destruction. Right from Bible times we would see that the Anointed were inventors and developed machines which they used in building.

Now we need to see into the minds of inventors. We should be reading the biography of Michael Faraday, a Christian whom I feel was an Anointed inventor, after the heart of God through whom we have electricity today, because he also provided light for the world:

'*Physicists and chemists alike look back on Faraday as a worthy pioneer, although his achievements in physics are the best known. He formulated the laws of electromagnetic induction and did the groundwork necessary to make dynamos, electric motors and transformers. It was Faraday who devised the laws of electrolysis and laid the foundation for the electroplating industry. Faraday has the international unit for capacitance named after him, the Farad, marking his distinguished work with dielectrics; and also a physical constant, the Faraday Constant. He developed the concept of magnetic and electrical fields, and also showed that the electrical phenomena exhibited by lightning, electric eels and voltaic cells are all related. The `Faraday dark space', observed with electrical discharges in gases (for example, as in fluorescent tubes), pays tribute to him, and the `Faraday effect' in magneto-optics was one of his triumphs later in his career. This list draws attention to just highlights in a life packed full of innovative discoveries.*

Most scientists would feel satisfied to make just one lasting contribution to their disciplines, but Faraday excelled in the quality and quantity of his output. It is natural for us to ask - how did he achieve all this? What made him tick? What motivated him? What kept him going? Many biographies disappoint because they restrict themselves to describing events that took place. We look for something a little deeper - what factors influenced Faraday as a human being and as a scientist?

Jim Baggott contributed a very perceptive article on Faraday to the 2nd September 1991 issue of New Scientist. After discussing aspects of this `man of genius', Baggott identifies religious belief as a key influence in Faraday's life.

`He was a devout member of the Sandemanian Church, a fundamentalist Christian order that demanded total faith and total commitment. Sandemanians organised their daily lives through their literal interpretation of the Bible. . .*

Faraday found no conflict between his religious beliefs and his activities as a scientist and philosopher. He viewed his discoveries of nature's laws as part of the continual process of `reading the book of nature', no different in principle from the process of reading the Bible to discover God's laws. A strong sense of the unity of God and nature pervaded Faraday's life and work.'

It is worth emphasising that his Christianity was wholehearted: Faraday loved to worship his God in the company of fellow-believers, and church meetings were a priority in his busy week. For many years, he was an elder in the fellowship, and he shared in the preaching of the Word of God.

Faraday's scientific world-view was deeply influenced by the message of the Bible. His belief in the unity of forces guided his experimental and theoretical research, and it linked with his belief in the unity of God.

The connection came because of his deep conviction that God's revelation of himself in creation is not unrelated to his revelation of himself in Scripture. Furthermore, Faraday knew that this universe is upheld by the mighty power of God...[1]

What made Faraday an Anointed inventor? It is the fact that he held God in high esteem, and as we have read, he was a devout Christian, an elder in fellowship for many years. Faraday's devout Christian beliefs influenced his work and he was devoted to his research. as he showed the unity of God and nature through his inventions, theories and discoveries. In another instance, it was reported that Faraday said on being asked about his afterlife expectation: *'I shall be with Christ, and that is enough.'*

Character of the Anointed inventor

From what we have discussed so far, we would at this juncture outline the character of an Anointed inventor, whose work adds value to living – given breath to dead situations, rather than inventing items that would destroy the peace of God on earth.

1. Fear of God: A God-fearing inventor would not invent instruments of war. This would be seen in Faraday's life: *'His religious beliefs may have been a reason he refused to help the British government's request that he might develop chemical weapons for the Crimean war.*[2]*'*

1. http://www.biblicalcreation.org.uk/educational_issues/bcs010.html
2. http://www.biographyonline.net/scientists/michael-faraday.html

2. Dependence on the wisdom of God: There is no life outside the wisdom of God. The Bible says in Jeremiah 8:9: 'The wise men are ashamed, they are dismayed and taken: lo, they have rejected the word of the Lord; and what wisdom is in them?' Any inventor who would not want to live a life of shame would certainly seek the wisdom of God.

3. Knowledge hungry: It was recorded of Michael Faraday: *'He was born on 22 September 1791 in south London to relatively poor parents. At the age of 14, he left school and started an apprenticeship at a local book binder. In his spare time he was an avid reader, teaching himself many scientific concepts. Faraday was thus mostly self-taught and became one of the greatest scientists despite his rudimentary maths In 1812, at the age of 20 he receive some tickets for a series of lectures by the eminent scientist Humphry Davy. After the lecture Michael sent Davy a 300 page document offering notes on the lectures. Davy was impressed and he employed Faraday as an assistant. This later led to a Fullerian Professor of Chemistry at the Royal Institution of Great Britain, a position to which he was appointed for life.*[2] His poor background did not deter him from seeking knowledge. Imagine an apprentice in bookbinding becoming the discoverer of electricity. Let's take a look at how he kept the details of Humphrey Davy's lecture and could write a 300-page document which Davy himself could not deny as a true account of his lectures.

This is the stamina of someone sent by the Anointing Order to give the earth physical light that they would relate with in their homes instead of burning fossil fuel in their lanterns. We need more inventors with the heart of God so that the world becomes a better place.

4. Deep thinker – The Bible tells us that in quietness and confidence shall be our strength (Isaiah 30:15). The Anointed inventor would be able to employ his ability to think deeply in the creation of things that would glorify God.

5. Patience – The beauty of experimenting: Michael Faraday said: '*Nothing is too wonderful to be true if it be consistent with the laws of nature, and in such things as these, experiment is the best test of such consistency.*' This was how he kept his heart on experimentation until he got through. An Anointed inventor is not moved by what he sees but what he expects to see. Anything short of that is not divine wisdom.

6. Confidence of eternity: Apart from the fear of God a person should be able to confirm in his/her heart that he/she will be with Jesus. This is what guides the Anointed inventor. His desire to get to heaven makes him tie his inventions to eternity and as such he is ready to satisfy God rather than man. His inventions would not take the world to the devil, but will give them the desire to repent and seek God.

Invention is about conquering your fears. Because the Lord has not given us the spirit of fear, we would say that the Anointed is an inventor. The Melchizedek Order is an Order of inventions as seen below:

Genesis 1:1 - *In the beginning, God created the heavens and the earth.*

Colossians 1:16-17 - *For by him were all things created, that are in heaven, and that are in earth, visible and invisible, whether they be thrones, or dominions, or principalities, or powers: all things were created by him, and for him: And he is before all things, and by him all things consist.*

So anyone Anointed by the Order must be a creator of things, visible and invincible as a result of the power of thoughtful imagination. The ability of the Anointed to create invincible things in his mind is what has culminated in all the inventions we see today. The Anointed inventor glorifies God with his inventions while the ordinary inventor glorifies satan with his inventions and takes people's hearts away from God through it.

CHAPTER SEVENTEEN

THE ANOINTED IN JUSTICE

If we have the Anointed in the seat of judgment, justice will prevail over wickedness, unlike what we see today in many of our law courts. Those who are judges in our law courts need to act in line and in principle with the command of God, to judge the fatherless (Isaiah 1:17), and this means doing justice to he who has no one to defend him, so as to vindicate his cause, without undermining his weak and vulnerable condition - his lack of knowledge and want of experience. Jesus is the judge of all. This shows that the work of a judge must be carried out by one who is spiritual, as truth is not found on the floor, and humans have a way of tainting the truth and sending the innocent to jail.

St. Paul said that the spiritual judges all things. When we hate evil, the Lord will come to seal us and consecrate us unto Himself: *'And said to him, 'Go throughout the city of Jerusalem and put a mark on the foreheads of those who grieve and lament over all the detestable things that are done in it.' As I listened, he said to the others, 'Follow him through the city and kill, without showing pity or compassion. Slaughter old men, young men and maidens, women and children, but do not touch anyone who has the mark. Begin at my sanctuary.' So they began with the elders who were in front of the temple* – Ezekiel 9:4-6 (NIV). This is where the Anointed judge comes in. He treasures salvation and would want to protect himself from destruction by standing for the truth all the time.

The Bible says: *And Jesus came and spake unto them, saying, All power is given unto me in heaven and in earth. There is one lawgiver, who is able to save and to destroy: who art thou that judgest another?* – Matthew 28:18, James 4:12. A look at the last statement in James 4:12 says: *who art thou that judgest another?* This shows that only one appointed by the Order has the right to judge the children of God as either a lawyer, a lawgiver – legislative arm of the government - or as a ruler. Only those who have the mind of Christ can give right judgment, because they would be receiving instructions from Him: *For who hath known the mind of the Lord, that he may instruct him?* – 1 Corinthians 2:16.

Those who have the mind of the Lord also have the law of the Lord written in their heart – Jeremiah 31:33, Hebrews 8:10: *I will put my laws into their mind, and write them in their hearts.* Any judge who would judge with the mind of Christ would not be led astray by mere facts cooked up to save the culprit and send the innocent to jail. The act of judgment is a spiritual act. And this implies that every court case is a spiritual affair, because it involves people's emotions, and these emotions create spiritual clouds in the vicinity of the place where the judgment is taking place. Thoughts are multiplied, heartbeats increase, people go into a trance or daydream, while many collapse.

This is not something to joke about. The future of an entire generation may become stale or be destroyed by that singular pronouncement of a jail sentence. This is the fact I want to present in this book. For instance, if Joseph had died in that prison, the nation of Egypt and all those who ran down, including his own family, during the famine would have perished. Yet Joseph was innocent. The way in which the rich and powerful in society have turned law institutions into defending them while silencing the voice of the less privileged in jail is the reason why anyone seeking to be a lawyer, a law giver or a judge must seek to know God so that God will instruct him/her so that their own judgment would not send them into everlasting torment in hell.

Solomon judged rightly in the case of the dead baby, because he was Anointed.

CHAPTER EIGHTTEEN

THE ANOINTED IN LEADERSHIP

Two of my earlier books, 'The Man God Made' and 'Leadership – An Eagle Eye Perspective', have dealt with this aspect of the Anointing character. For instance, in my leadership book I started off by explaining that the true leader is a leader who acts as the second hand of the clock which painstakingly does its job without complaint. For every cycle it runs, it adds beauty to our aspirations in life.

All we have been talking about as the exploits of the Anointed points to leadership. The Melchizedek Order is a leadership order. And a study of the entire books of the Bible points to leadership. The beauty of the leadership character in the Order is seen in the hierarchical organization that exists therein.

Here I will recommend that you see my other two books mentioned above. But before we leave this chapter, I would want to say that the Anointed Leader is one who obeys the oath he takes in public before those he leads. We would see

King Saul's leadership crashing after the oath he entered with his soldiers was broken by his own son in 1 Samuel 14. Now let's see this; Jonathan broke an oath he wasn't aware of and Saul wanted him dead. Now in 1 Samuel 15 Saul pleaded for forgiveness after disobeying God, can you imagine?

The Bible says that whatever we do unto others, so also shall we be treated. We are also told that the merciful shall obtain mercy.

When Samuel mourned for Saul at the end of the day after his offence of disobedience against God, did that change the heart of God? No! God indeed raised a new leader (1 Samuel 16:1). Every leader must be guided on this fact - that once they disobey God's instructions, they are heading for their downfall. This is where the Anointed leader with the fear of God will excel. More of this you would see in the two books recommended earlier, if you want to grow your leadership gift.

CHAPTER NINETEEN

FURTHER HUMAN ENDEAVOURS

Now that we have discussed some of the fields of exploits, in this chapter we will discuss some other specific careers and how someone with the anointing of the Lord, whose heart yearns for the things of God, can function without having to offend God and then hew curses upon him/her.

The Anointed in sport

Sports have become careers to so many people. Often when there is a season of sporting activities, I have seen sports fans abandon church services. Many pastors have had to turn their churches to where people would gather to watch sports as if in a cinema before weekly church services so that they can attract sports enthusiasts to come to the service. This tells us the influence sport is having on the people.

Is it wrong to be a sports enthusiast? I don't think so. What we are discussing here will enable those who choose sport as a career to excel, and their fans will also understand that God is the reason for man's ability to carry out sporting activities, and that the non-recognition of God in their lives is sin. St. Paul advised in 1Timothy 4:8-9: *For bodily exercise profiteth little: but godliness is profitable unto all things, having promise of the life that now is, and of that which is to come. This is a faithful saying and worthy of all acceptation.*

Why would Paul advise such a thing? It could be seen in his complaints about Demas, who he said had gone after the world.

I have seen people who jog daily trying to burn up fat, but these same people would find it difficult to become involved in the works of evangelism, or even undergo a fasting and prayer exercise for the sake of the work of God. Many have died from sporting activities. Others have being maimed for life by injuries sustained in practice and in competition, but how many of them have had to experience this for the sake of the gospel?

I agree that sporting events can bring unity among brethren for the purpose of doing the will of God, and this is where the Anointed comes into play. I have read how sporting festivals were once occasions when Christians were devoured by wild animals which were trained and kept for that purpose in Rome in their amphitheatres, which we see today as masterpieces of human wisdom but often forget the evil that went on inside them against the work of God.

While many of us have frowned upon this act, we have also, during sporting events, locked the word of God in the morgue until the festive period was over. During this period satanic acts increase – prostitution, stealing, defrauding, etc. Most football clubs are owned and sponsored by occult people.

So anyone anointed who is a sport enthusiast should ensure that they are not led astray. They should always remember that associating themselves with evil will only lead them to hell, because evil communication corrupts good manners (1 Corinthians 15:33). We should not forget that once in the Bible, the devil initiated the move by men to gather in order to dishonour God's will for man to subdue and fill the earth while trying to build the tower of Babel (Genesis 11). Today we should see most sporting festivals as gatherings that have not been done to honour God. Let us think about it. As one with the fear of God at heart, let your involvement in sports not take you away from God, but be an avenue for evangelizing.

The Anointed in the medical profession

Saving lives is the ultimate goal of the medical profession. Many believers have become doctors or are functioning in paramedical careers. The purpose of this section is to guide such a person, to ensure that their medical practice does not take them to hell.

An anointed medical professional should see his/her career as one to help encourage people to value life physically and spiritually. Since they already have an understanding of the human anatomy, they would also no doubt be able to use their expertise to convince people of the existence of a Holy God. Even as they rush to save a life in an emergency, they should become bearers of the 'good news' of salvation and be involved in encouraging or training evangelists and teachers of the word of God to enable them to win souls, as many are already heading for eternal destruction in hell.

Over time, some in the medical profession have been bedeviled by occult men and women who use their profession as a channel to take life and drain blood into the blood bank of satan. Even so, the Anointed should use his/her profession in medicine to save life and protect his/her patient from spiritual attacks through the receipt of revelation from God. This is implying that the anointed medical professional should seek to grow in the pursuit of spiritual awakening, with the power of the Holy Spirit and a gift of prophecy to be able to function successfully in this calling. The Anointed should not forget that God has kept him/her there and enabled him/her to succeed in his/her chosen career because he/she is to become God's instrument of restoration there and to teach his/her colleagues the way of the Lord. So instead of seeing himself/herself as a medical professional, he/she should rather see that function as God sending them there for the purpose of rescue.

The Anointed Designer

Beauty is the heart of creation. A designer would not want to offend God. Anyone whose work of design will corrupt people's hearts is an agent of the devil. Whether you are a fashion designer or practising architectural or engineering design, you should be able to judge with your heart the effect of what you are designing on people's imaginations and their unity with the purpose of God in their lives. If we foresee the devil influencing their lives negatively as a result of our designs, we should not go ahead.

A designer often works by inspiration, which later becomes realistic imagination. This further points to the fact that the art of designing and drawing is controlled by spiritual forces. This is why in the design and fashioning of the Tabernacle, God advised Moses in Exodus 31:2-11, to use only those He had inspired:

2   *See, I have called by name Bezaleel the son of Uri, the son of Hur, of the tribe of Judah:*

3   *And I have filled him with the spirit of God, in wisdom, and in understanding, and in knowledge, and in all manner of workmanship,*

4 *To devise cunning works, to work in gold, and in silver, and in brass,*

5 *And in cutting of stones, to set them, and in carving of timber, to work in all manner of workmanship.*

6 *And I, behold, I have given with him Aholiab, the son of Ahisamach, of the tribe of Dan: and in the hearts of all that are wise hearted I have put wisdom, that they may make all that I have commanded thee;*

7 *The tabernacle of the congregation, and the ark of the testimony, and the mercy seat that is thereupon, and all the furniture of the tabernacle,*

8 *And the table and his furniture, and the pure candlestick with all his furniture, and the altar of incense,*

9 *And the altar of burnt offering with all his furniture, and the laver and his foot,*

10 *And the cloths of service, and the holy garments for Aaron the priest, and the garments of his sons, to minister in the priest's office,*

11 *And the anointing oil, and sweet incense for the holy place: according to all that I have commanded thee shall they do.*

This also points to the fact that anyone possessed by the satanic spirit will be filled with satanic wisdom to design items that will take hearts away from God. This they will do all the time they are involve in design activities, like carving of images for idolatry. The anointed designer should see his/her career as an evangelical tool to win hearts to God. Such designs should focus on replicating heavenly values of honour unto God here on earth, and not things representing obscenity.

The Anointed in Engineering

I am an engineer by profession, and came to it as a result of my studies at university. Engineering adds value to the life we live here on earth, and a look at the world show us myriads of engineering masterpieces. While many of these have been done with good intentions, others were done with the intention of oppression, which is against what Jesus came to die for. An Anointed engineer, as what we have said over and over, is one who is mindful of the effect of the works of his/her creation, ensuring that by and large, it is done to honour God and not to abuse God's creation or trying to prove a point to convince people of the non-existence of God.

A look at the same Exodus 31:2-11 we read in our earlier discussion shows us elements of engineering - implying that the spirit of God can actually enable one to succeed as an engineer. My advice is that no engineer should allow his or her professional drive to take them to hell. The anointed engineer should therefore imbibe the principles we have been discussing - seeking the wisdom of God before accepting an engineering job. Even in companies, once the Anointed perceives satanic acts such as cheating and fraudulent practices like using poor quality materials in order to increase profit margin, he/she should speak out and advise whoever is involved to desist. If truly the anointing is speaking for you, you would be respected. Those who would try to blacklist you so that you are sacked will not see the light of day. I have heard of several testimonies of people who would have been involved in such practices who refused and the Lord promoted them. So do not forsake God while trying to protect your career. Let integrity guide your heart always.

The Anointed in Science

The theory of evolution has done a lot of damage to the world and society. Biologists even say that humans should be classified as an animal, against the Biblical proof that indeed man only wears a form that makes him have the characteristics of other living beings, but bears the image and likeness of God. We have seen all around the world how man has acted as God's voice. Would a being who communed with God be an animal? I don't think so.

There are various scientific experiments which have affected the world negatively. An anointed scientist will not be involved in scientific practices that would cause damage, as nuclear power has done in recent times. While it is good to carry out scientific quests, we should not also forget that most of these quests are masterminds of the devil aimed at discrediting what God is doing.

Albert Einstein, Nobel Laureate in Physics 1921, once said: 'The more I study science the more I believe in God.'

The Anointed in Financial Management

It is an easy thing for those in this profession to commit fraud and many would think that paying a tithe of what is stolen is acceptable before God. Fraudulent acts should be discouraged. The Anointed must ensure he/she is not involved in fraudulent practices.

The Anointed in Governance

The beauty of governance is when it becomes an art that sees through the hearts of people, painting their needs on a tablet. Governance is the combination of acts of leadership and administration. I have decided to discuss this separately because of some salient characters I want to explain which will make everyone in governance succeed. In order to understand what we are discussing, I want us to have properly digested all we have been discussing since, because the people who are governed are made up of the professions and many more not discussed here. The Anointed in government sees the heart of these professionals and sees how he/she can help to bring out the best in them for the growth and development of society in the fear of the Lord.

CHAPTER TWENTY

SEEKING SPECIFIC ANOINTING

The Israelites prayed that Prophet Elias (Elijah) should come because the Lord said he would herald the coming of the saviour: *Behold, I will send you Elijah the prophet before the coming of the great and dreadful day of the Lord* – Malachi 4:5, and Jesus confirmed to His disciples that 'John the Baptist' was the Elias they have been expecting - Matthew 11:12-14; 17:12. Every anointing specifies a job to be done: *Behold, I will send my messenger, and he shall prepare the way before me: and the Lord, whom ye seek, shall suddenly come to his temple…* Malachi 3:1, so as to bring to pass the thought of God towards us – the thought of Good and not of Evil in order to bring us to an expected end of prosperity, peace, unity and love.

What people call reincarnation is actually the replication of anointing. Moses transferred wisdom to Joshua through the laying on of hands. Elijah transferred a double portion of his anointing to Elisha through a mantle. Today you can still seek this anointing because the Holy Spirit which made it possible then now lives with us, unlike in their time when He would only come upon them in due season, as ordained by the Order.

We can actually seek specific anointing as we had seen in the exploits of any of the Anointed servants of God in the Bible. We all know that Jesus is the same yesterday, today and forever – Hebrews 13:8, which defines the existence of God as, the 'I am that I am' – Exodus 3:14. This implies that the anointing of old is still available for us if we would seek it, so that we may have more Elijah, Elisha, Daniel, Joseph, Peter, Paul, John the Baptist, John the brother of Jesus who revealed the book of Revelation, Deborah, and so on.

To pray that God should give you any of these anointings, you need to understand what your purpose on earth is. This usually shows in the gifts of the Holy Spirit you display. Once you know it, you can ask for the same spirit that was upon them. We can have an explanation to this from the book of Isaiah 61:1 - *The Spirit of the Lord God is upon me, because the Lord has Anointed me to bring good news to the poor; he has sent me to bind up the brokenhearted...*, and compare it with Jesus confirmation in Luke 4:18, that this is exactly what He came to do. The Holy Spirit is the same, and if Jesus would indeed live in us as we often profess, then in line with 1 Corinthians 1:24, we would all be filled with the Power and Wisdom of God. Instead of wasting our time binding and casting out devils, we should pray for the infilling of the Holy Spirit. This of course has to do with how ready we are to build our faith in God through the hearing, studying and imbibing the word of God. And because the word of God is the Spirit of God, gradually we would begin to grow into the awareness of living an upright life before God in all that we would do.

From this premise we would explain some anointing in the Bible that we can seek. Jesus says, ask and you will receive, seek and you will find. It is time to ask and seek, because the anointing makes the difference.

Joseph's anointing

We can understand his kind of anointing from his dreams: *And he said unto them, Hear, I pray you, this dream which I have dreamed: For, behold, we were binding sheaves in the field, and, lo, my sheaf arose, and also stood upright; and, behold, your sheaves stood round about, and made obeisance to my sheaf. And his brethren said to him, Shalt thou indeed reign over us? or shalt thou indeed have dominion over us? And they hated him yet the more for his dreams, and for his words. And he dreamed yet another dream, and told it his brethren, and said, Behold, I have dreamed a dream more; and, behold, the sun and the moon and the eleven stars made obeisance to me. And he told it to his father, and to his brethren: and his father rebuked him, and said unto him, what is this dream that thou hast dreamed? Shall I and thy mother and thy brethren indeed come to bow down ourselves to thee to the earth? And his brethren envied him; but his father observed the saying* – Genesis 37:6-11. From this we would see that the Joseph's anointing is an anointing of:.

- Leadership with authority of influence – the head and not the tail

- Envy, as people will hate anyone with the anointing because of the greatness they would see around him.

- Prosperity as a result of the position of trust the Anointed occupies.

Anyone who is in Christ can desire this anointing and it will be apportioned unto him. The anointing of Joseph was also at play in the life of Daniel, but the Daniel's anointing spells excellence, which was a peculiar attribute in his life as a result of his fellowship with God.

Elijah's anointing

We can see the basic character of Elijah's anointing from 1 Kings 19:14: *And he said, I have been very jealous for the Lord God of hosts: because the children of Israel have forsaken thy covenant, thrown down thine altars, and slain thy prophets with the sword.* We would also see this in the life of John the Baptist. John once said: *But when he saw many of the Pharisees and Sadducees come to his baptism, he said unto them, O generation of vipers, who hath warned you to flee from the wrath to come?* Now, compare this with Elijah's statement above. Both of them were sent to confront the sins in the lives of the Israelites. Anyone desiring this anointing must be ready to confront evil all the time.

Solomon's anointing

Solomon possessed such strength that was in display in his governance. He had wisdom and was far-sighted - a quality which made it possible for him to complete the temple building project.

Zerubbabel's anointing

There are people who God uses to repair the wreckage in society and the church. Zerubbabel is one of such people. As a governor in the land of Judah, his first desire after hearing the word of the Lord was to obey God and rebuilding His temple, so that the children of Israel would again gather to bless God. Today, with the decay we have in society and church, we need more of Zerubbabel and Nehemiah to set things right (the books of Ezra and Haggai). Another anointing that fits in here is that of Hezekiah who reinstated temple worship after a long period of neglect (2 Chronicles 29).

Job's anointing

A look at the book of Job 29 will tell us what sort of man Job was. These qualities were what moved God to become so proud of him that he was seen by the Order as: *... none like him in the earth, a perfect and an upright man, one that feareth God, and escheweth evil?* – Job 1:8. His qualities are:

- Unique and outstanding
- Upright
- Fears God
- Avoids evil

Specific verses that tell of this man's walk with God are seen in Job 29 verses 12,14,15,16, 17, 21 below:

- 'Because I delivered the poor that cried, and the fatherless, and him that had none to help him.'
- 'I put on righteousness, and it clothed me: my judgment was as a robe and a diadem.'
- 'I was eyes to the blind, and feet was I to the lame.'
- 'I was a father to the poor: and the cause which I knew not I searched out.'
- 'And I brake the jaws of the wicked, and plucked the spoil out of his teeth.'
- 'Unto me men gave ear, and waited, and kept silence at my counsel.'

In effect, Job was doing what God does every day. This is

what Jesus also was doing, which He says is exactly what the Father was doing in heaven. And if we would do this, then we would be as perfect as God. Anyone desiring to have these qualities can ask God, and such a person should use Job 29 as his/her watchword. It is possible to be like Job - someone who will not curse God no matter the ugly situation he/she may be facing.

Mary's anointing

Mary found favour with God and was used as a holy vessel for the work of God, bearing Jesus in her womb. She must have possessed distinguishing attributes which made her most favoured among all the daughters of Israel. Every young lady should desire the kind of anointing that she bore.

Sarah's anointing

Sarah endured her marriage even when she was denied by her husband, Abraham, for fear of being attacked by Pharaoh and Abimelech. All married women need Sarah's spirit and should use her godly life as a role model to be able to endure the trials that come with their marriage.

Hannah's anointing

The anointing upon Hannah – the mother of Samuel - is special in her ability to seek the face of God and to fulfill her vow to Him. The other Hannah is the widow who served God for 84 years as a prophetess. Don't forget also that the mother of Samuel also prophesied. So the Hannah's anointing is an anointing of fulfilling vows, prophesying and serving the Lord whole heartedly.

Anointing is a burden we bear for the Lord, so that we may complete the specific task it is set to accomplish. This is what Jesus meant when He said that we should take His yoke upon us and learn of Him. The more we study the Bible the more we come across more anointing that we can desire and then ask from the Lord. Jesus says: *Hitherto have ye asked nothing in my name: ask, and ye shall receive, that your joy may be full -* John 16:24. Asking for the Holy Spirit is not enough; you need to know what gift of the Holy Spirit you need to help you achieve your targets in life, then you go through the Bible and know those who worked for God were in similar profession and what they did. This will help you understand their own temptations and the reason(s) why they may not have kept their service to God in sanctity. Once you have this with you, you can start the asking process. And God will certainly not give you anything less: *If ye then, being evil, know how to give good gifts unto your children, how much more shall your Father which is in heaven give good things to them that ask him? -* Matthew 7:11

What you desire is what you get. What you appreciate is

what comes to you. What you admire is what takes your attention. What you love is what lives in you. How did I receive the gift of writing so that today I can write a book in under a month? I desired, admired, and love the Anointed servants of God, who write, and I got some of their books, went to the altar and prayed for the gift. Today the gift lives in me because I love the act of writing.

We chose the kinds of courses and the universities we attended. Sometimes our parents or guardian did. This is how it is with our lives. How we live our lives rests on the choice we make daily. Our God is the same yesterday, today and forever. Therefore, the same anointing of old which makes those in the Bible to do exploit in His name is still available.

CHAPTER TWENTY ONE

HOW TO SEEK ANOINTING

Nicodemus went to meet Jesus secretly to seek anointing – which was what he needed to be saved. This is how it works. Every vessel requesting to be filled must first be emptied and cleaned. This is actually what the Holy Spirit does in our lives, teaching us the way of the Lord so that we may receive Him when He comes in.

There is always a way out of every situation you are experiencing. This is why Jesus says we should hand over our burden to Him and take His yoke upon us. What many of us have done is abandon what God says we should do, and we are busy doing what He should have done for us, which is impossible within human judgment. But with God all things are possible, so wisdom should inform us to let God have His way in our lives, using us as His instruments in His vineyard while He takes over our burden. This is what your employer does for you. You receive wages for the effort you put into His work, which takes away your financial burden.

There are rules for everything we do on earth. Rules are meant to bring the best out of an individual within a circle he/she subscribes to. They may be stringent and difficult to obey or live with. The more tasking they are, the better the reward. To succeed in life means you must adhere to rules that lead to success. The utmost rule to success is seeking God's anointing (Psalm 89:20). In the session that follows we will be discussing what we needed to know about the seeking of the anointing.

Substance of the Anointing

A substance is something you can hold; it is a support, just like a walking stick. It is like a vehicle that transports you without your needing to stress yourself walking to your intended destination, to bring you to an expected end.

Anointing is God's design to take away your burden of hopelessness. It is help from God. We see in the Bible that the moment the Levitical Order was instituted by God, these humans could do all things – from supervision of the tabernacle and the temple building to playing musical instruments and singing praises to God. Anointing not put to use is 'redundant anointing', whereas an anointing that is put into use and is achieving results is 'exercised anointing.' An exercised anointing may have been fully or partially exercised.

A fully exercised anointing achieves more through networking with other people with similar anointing, through reading their stories or through physical contact with them, so that they tell you their own experiences to guide you. People can also have multiple anointing characters when they have the fullness of the seven spirits of God, in which case they become the vision drivers while using others to achieve the task associated with each of these anointings. A partially exercised anointing, as the name implies, is one which has not been fully utilized to achieve what God intended it for. We have heard of unfulfilled destiny. This is how partially exercised anointing works.

Stages of the Anointing

In the revelation I received on the 18th January 2009, it was revealed to me that the anointing are in two stages: the main anointing and the supporting anointing. Without the supporting anointing the main anointing cannot yield the intended results. Satan will usually attack sources of the supporting anointing so that our main anointing does not blossom. This is why we often begin to have discord with people who meant well for us. The poor in most cases gossip and hate the rich, who may possess the wisdom that they would have received and get out of poverty.

Main Anointing

The evident of this anointing can be seen in Psalms 22:10: *I was cast upon thee from the womb: thou art my God from my mother's belly*.

Before many of us were born our parents had already influenced our main anointing. Parents have a lot to do with our destiny because of the type of religion they practised and where we were born. Many of us were delivered in witch-doctors' maternity. Also, the souls of many children have been mortgaged by their parents due to the kind of oath they entered into with witch-doctors. For instance, even when Solomon was successful, the foundation was ungodly - his mother was another man's wife.

There is what is called spiritual transmutation and infusion. People can be affected by spiritual invocations which affects the way many reason and do the sort of things they do. The anointing character is seen easily in our day to day lives, which means that the character we exhibit is a direct reflection of the anointing we bear – godly or evil. We can see an example of what the main anointing carries from Jacob's prophetic prayers in Genesis 29: 3-27:

*3 **Reuben**, thou art my firstborn, my might, and the beginning of my strength, the excellency of dignity, and the excellency of power: 4 Unstable as water, thou shalt not excel; because thou wentest up to thy father's bed; then defiledst thou it: he went up to my couch.*

5 **Simeon** and **Levi** are brethren; instruments of cruelty are in their habitations. 6 O my soul, come not thou into their secret; unto their assembly, mine honor, be not thou united: for in their anger they slew a man, and in their self-will they digged down a wall. 7 Cursed be their anger, for it was fierce; and their wrath, for it was cruel: I will divide them in Jacob, and scatter them in Israel.

8 **Judah**, thou art he whom thy brethren shall praise: thy hand shall be in the neck of thine enemies; thy father's children shall bow down before thee. 9 Judah is a lion's whelp: from the prey, my son, thou art gone up: he stooped down, he couched as a lion, and as an old lion; who shall rouse him up? 10 The sceptre shall not depart from Judah, nor a lawgiver from between his feet, until Shiloh come; and unto him shall the gathering of the people be. 11 Binding his foal unto the vine, and his ass's colt unto the choice vine; he washed his garments in wine, and his clothes in the blood of grapes: 12 His eyes shall be red with wine, and his teeth white with milk.

13 **Zebulun** shall dwell at the haven of the sea; and he shall be for an haven of ships; and his border shall be unto Zidon.

14 **Issachar** is a strong ass couching down between two burdens: 15 And he saw that rest was good, and the land that it was pleasant; and bowed his shoulder to bear, and became a servant unto tribute.

16 **Dan** shall judge his people, as one of the tribes of Israel. 17 Dan shall be a serpent by the way, an adder in the path, that biteth

the horse heels, so that his rider shall fall backward. 18 I have waited for thy salvation, O Lord.

19 **Gad***, a troop shall overcome him: but he shall overcome at the last.*

20 Out of **Asher** *his bread shall be fat, and he shall yield royal dainties.*

21 **Naphtali** *is a hind let loose: he giveth goodly words.*

22 **Joseph** *is a fruitful bough, even a fruitful bough by a well; whose branches run over the wall: 23 The archers have sorely grieved him, and shot at him, and hated him: 24 But his bow abode in strength, and the arms of his hands were made strong by the hands of the mighty God of Jacob; (from thence is the shepherd, the stone of Israel:) 25 Even by the God of thy father, who shall help thee; and by the Almighty, who shall bless thee with blessings of heaven above, blessings of the deep that lieth under, blessings of the breasts, and of the womb: 26 The blessings of thy father have prevailed above the blessings of my progenitors unto the utmost bound of the everlasting hills: they shall be on the head of Joseph, and on the crown of the head of him that was separate from his brethren.*

27 **Benjamin** *shall raven as a wolf: in the morning he shall devour the prey, and at night he shall divide the spoil.*

From these we would see that these children were born of the same father, grew up and raised in the same home. Where then did all the characters seen come from? Some were good and honourable, while others were bad and disgracefully shameful. Simply say some were carrying a faulty main anointing, enshrined with the devil's intent from the womb. Every child born into these tribes will be fused from birth with the spirits the above statements from Jacob carries.

Substance of the main Anointing

- We are born with it

- It is loaded with supernatural information – which people can see and tell you what the child will achieve on earth. The angels always said this when they come to deliver a message about the birth of a child – e.g. the message of Samson, John the Baptist, and Jesus. Before Isaac was born God had decreed that he would inherit Abraham's blessings - whether Isaac liked it or not, God's anointing was there for him from the womb. Even in the case of Esau and Jacob, Go decided to love Jacob. And this love is the main anointing he bears. All firstborn belongs to God, it is already there and nothing changes that.

- They contain your birthday and the day you will die. A reference to this will be seen in the following verses: Job 14:5 – *'Seeing his days are determined, the number of his months are with thee, thou hast appointed his bounds that he cannot pass'* and in Exodus 23:26 – *'I will fulfill the number of your days.'* This is why those who have spiritual eyes always tell you it is time or not time, because they can check the information packets existing in your life. It contains who will be your parents. It controls how you will eventually grow in life. This is why in most cases, no matter what happens to us, we end up finally becoming who God wants us to be.

- Inherit generational curses and until these are cleared, the supporting anointing cannot take its root.
- Inherit generational blessings also – eg Abraham to Isaac.

Supporting Anointing

This is your own duty. You are the one to work this out. This includes the training we receive from our parents or guardian. We are also schooled in specific professions and we learn to grow even better in our individual gifts. The Bible tells us of Samson – no razor was to touch his hair as a condition to allow the main anointing to manifest. The moment the razor came upon his hair, he lost the strength that characterized the power in his main anointing.

The coat of many colours of Joseph also announced the purpose of his main anointing. If the main anointing is faulty the supporting anointing can do nothing, as the Bible says: *what can the righteous do if the foundation is destroyed* (Psalms 11:3) – the main anointing is the foundation.

Substance of the supporting Anointing

■ The wisdom we receive daily teaches us how to lead our lives successfully and to avoid people who will lead you astray, to repent and show remorse after we commit sin, enabling our conscience to be alive.

■ The supporting anointing releases God's blessings to the measure in our main anointing, because we are already informed and know what purpose we were created for on earth.

■ King David's earlier encounter with music brought him into the king's palace. Then his warlord nature sprang forth, as he killed wild animals which came devouring his father's flocks. And later he became a king, building a city, becoming a prominent King after the heart of God. From here we would say that his main character was from the womb, which is why he said that he was fearfully and wonderfully made by God, then the supporting anointing came into being when Samuel anointed him, and from that time he received favour to be recommended to be the one who would play the harp that would eventually calm Saul, because he was carrying the anointing of the Lord. It is only the anointing of God that can chase evil spirits away, and that was exactly what happened to Saul as David became a possessor of the anointed arm of God.

■ As you come across knowledge of God daily, you will begin

to receive insight on how to retrace your path back to your destiny. The supporting anointing helps to re-ignite your hopes and dreams. This may happen through testimonies of others, prayers, laying of hands from an anointed servant of God, training, mentoring, etc. The word of the Lord is a lamp upon our feet.

Faulty Main Anointing

The main anointing could become faulty. A fault in something has to do with something going wrong out of the intended. Many of us have a fault in our main anointing or path to our destiny. Our purpose in life becomes unclear, obscured and fuzzy. This often shows up in our dreams; we find ourselves in forests, graves, accidents, chased by wild animals or we often wake up crying out of our dreams into the physical. When we experienced these or similar dreams we should know that the path to our Destiny is not well mapped out. Some people's main anointing is enshrined in wickedness because of mutilation by devil - Psalm 58:3, which could be occasioned by the wickedness of the parent or polluted by witch-doctors.

Restoring Faulty Main Anointing
- Receive the gospel – Matthew 11:5, Luke 4:18
- Accept Jesus today and repent – Mark 1:15

- Write down the areas you have failed to enable you know that you have a burden you must hand over to Jesus – Matthew 11:28

- Seek deliverance this moment by renouncing every evil association or acts you have engaged in – Matthew 8:28-29

- Pray for the Lord to blot out any curse(s) in your family and in your life – Isaiah 1:18, Exodus 26:5

- Hope and trust in God's ability to make all things right in your life in His own time and due season – Jeremiah 17:7

- Live for God alone – Matthew 19:21, Mark 6:12; 12:43

CHAPTER
TWENTY TWO

EXERCISING THE ANOINTING ORDER CHARACTER

We need to recap the verses of the Scripture that springs up our quest for this Anointing Order and what we intend to gain by subscribing to the Order. These are:

■ **Hebrews 5:9-10:** *'And being made perfect, he became the author of eternal salvation unto all them that obey him; called of God an high priest after the order of Melchizedek.'*

■ **Hebrews 6:19-20:** *'Which hope we have as an anchor of the soul, both sure and steadfast, and which entereth into that within the veil; whither the forerunner is for us entered, even Jesus, made an high priest for ever after the order of Melchizedek.'*

■ **Hebrews 7:1-3:** *'For this Melchizedek, king of Salem, priest of the most high God, who met Abraham returning from the slaughter of the kings, and blessed him; To whom also Abraham* *gave a tenth part of all; first being by interpretation King of righteousness, and after that also King of Salem, which is, King of peace; Without father, without mother, without descent, having neither beginning of days, nor end of life; but made like unto the Son of God; abideth a priest continually.'*

■ **Hebrews 7:26-28:** *'For such an high priest became us, who is holy, harmless, undefiled, separate from sinners, and made higher than the heavens; Who needeth not daily, as those high priests, to offer up sacrifice, first for his own sins, and then for the people's: for this he did once, when he offered up himself. For the law maketh men high priests which have infirmity; but the word of the oath, which was since the law, maketh the Son, who is consecrated for evermore.'*

The fact of care and provision from the Order as captured in Hebrews 7:26-28 is the reason we need this anointing.

■ You will not visit prophets to see for you, because you are going to see.
■ You will know how to pray and seek the face of God.
■ You will become zealous for the things of God.
■ You will become like Jesus, who was never sick.
■ You will be announced in whatever you do because Jesus was announced as heir of the Order, and being Anointed

after his stead will connect you to the Order as joint heirs to the Kingdom of El Elyon.

■ You will eat the wealth of the Land, including the possessions of the Gentiles, as they now work for you, as captured in Isaiah 61:6.

But before you can benefit from all these, you need to answer the Altar call. Before we continue, if you have not been accepted by the Order, there is no way the exercise below will benefit you. Now, if you are that person, say: Lord Jesus I repent of my sins – I believe you are my Lord and personal Saviour – come and dwell in me – fill me with the Power and the Wisdom of God. Thank you for receiving me today. Amen! You are done.

Now we move ahead into the next action.

It is time for serious business, because the violent taketh it by force - those who know their right in Christ cannot remain calm anymore while the enemy takes ownership of their destiny. Let us get ready for His Spirit this moment - Let's sanctify our body by confessing our sins - Let's open our hearts to accept Him

We need to see what transpired between the widow and the representative of the Melchizedek Order in 2 Kings 4:1-6: '*Now there cried a certain woman of the wives of the sons of the prophets unto Elisha, saying, Thy servant my husband is dead;*

and thou knowest that thy servant did fear the Lord: and the creditor is come to take unto him my two sons to be bondmen. And Elisha said unto her, What shall I do for thee? tell me, what hast thou in the house? And she said, Thine handmaid hath not any thing in the house, save a pot of oil. Then he said, Go, borrow thee vessels abroad of all thy neighbours, even empty vessels; borrow not a few. And when thou art come in, thou shalt shut the door upon thee and upon thy sons, and shalt pour out into all those vessels, and thou shalt set aside that which is full. So she went from him, and shut the door upon her and upon her sons, who brought the vessels to her; and she poured out. And it came to pass, when the vessels were full, that she said unto her son, Bring me yet a vessel. And he said unto her, There is not a vessel more. And the oil stayed.'

In the Order complaints are not accepted, what the Order understands is captured in Elisha's action in 2 Kings 2:13-14: *'He took up also the mantle of Elijah that fell from him, and went back, and stood by the bank of Jordan; And he took the mantle of Elijah that fell from him, and smote the waters, and said, Where is the Lord God of Elijah? and when he also had smitten the waters, they parted hither and thither: and Elisha went over.'*

Decrees upon decrees, action and action, say it, keep on saying it – that is what is understood. What you say is what is established for you – including your deepest thoughts. It is an Order where everything is possible, so instead of complaining, get into the Order through the anointing and obedience to every commandment from the Order and the Order will take over you burden.

Key facts from the Scripture we just read:

☐ She lost the link to the Order once her husband died and life had become difficult for her and her sons.

☐ Her two sons are about to become slaves to labour and suffering, which would bring about her untimely death because of loneliness and lack of help.

☐ Elisha's question is what the Order does - you are the one to say what you require from the Order. Jesus says up till now you have not asked - they have been praying, but have not asked for the deeper things. So the Holy Spirit is needed to take them into the archive of knowledge and wisdom.

☐ The second question from the Order representative standing before her and her needs was: 'what have thou in the house?' God multiplies what you have with you. So what do you want God to multiply today? Use the anointing on it - today is a day of prophetic manifestation. Do not sit down. You must decree the life you want to see after now. It is time to stand against every Altar of Melchiresha with the Anointing in you. The oil jar with her was her weapon against poverty and want. The staff of Moses was his own weapon. You have a job? That is your weapon against stagnation. You have a husband? God must bless him to take the house from poverty. You have a certificate? That is an instrument for success. What is in your hand? Every time I tell God to bless me with the spirit of writing and use the books as instruments to reach His children so that they will make heaven and also use them to take me out of poverty and want.

Not until she had no more empty vessels the oil kept flowing – what is limiting you? If we have the mind of being a blessing to others and making this world a better place, we would abhor whatever the Order hates and become united with it, in principles and actions.

After asking the Lord to forgive you your sins, check in your own heart also that you are not having grudges against anybody. Then stand facing the EAST as the sun rises this morning. Say: *Lord I stand facing your Holy Temple upon Mount Zion this morning that you may reign over me.* You should pray to receive the Melchizedek Anointing. Say: *Lord fill me with Melchizedek anointing -the anointing to decree things to pass. Fill me with you spirit this morning. Anoint your head with oil. And say Lord possess me with the Melchizedek Anointing.* Sincerely let God know you desire His innermost filling.

You will then begin to act as the violent referred to in Matthew 11:12: 'From the days of John the Baptist until now the kingdom of heaven suffers violence, and violent men take it by force.' Start to decree things to pass:

- ☐ In your home - peace, provisions, against shame, against death.
- ☐ In your marriage - lay your hand on your marriage picture and decree.
- ☐ On your children - lay a hand upon them and they will receive spiritual illumination.
- ☐ On your business - go into your store as you conclude this prayer and begin to chase out every spiritual cankerworm eating your business.
- ☐ Lay your hand upon your brain and decree intelligence and remembrance. Never will you forget anything again. It is time to shine in your academics.
- ☐ Rub your body with the anointing oil and decree good health upon your life - no more sickness, decree favour and command of influence.

Stretch forth your hand and speak into your future. There are no limits, because the Order is limitless.

The widow obeyed the instructions of the prophet and her increase came. As you obey the voice from this chapter may God, even the God of Abraham, Isaac, and Jacob, even the God who called me, may He not deny you increase on every side. Amen.

CHAPTER
TWENTY THREE

HOW TO REMAIN ANOINTED

Love what God loves to remain relevant, because people want God to solve their problems, and so if God would reveal answers to people's problems through you, you would be sought after. This is how we can remain in the anointing. As the Lord's glory is revealed through you daily, in your acts, you would also discover that your burden will be taken away and replaced with the joy of the Lord that now fills your heart.

As for you, the anointing you received from him remains in you, and you do not need anyone to teach you. But as his anointing teaches you about all things and as that anointing is real, not counterfeit—just as it has taught you, remain in him. – 1 John 2:27 (NIV)

Desire to grow the anointing
Shortly after my ministry started and the church was born, the Lord told me that I would undergo a compulsory and

mandatory six years of training and tutelage from the Anointing Order. That was in October 2008. I was terrified – six whole years! I gasped. Then He started me on this journey. As at 31st of July 2012 while I am writing this book, the tenth book after the release of my first book in November 2009, I could feel the strength of the anointing stronger than how it was when I started in 2008. The anointing enabled me to get people together to help me build and work in the ministry – developed training materials for the school of ministry, conceived and supervised the building of a worship centre that can house about 800 persons in the second year, and the church is growing strong by the day.

How did we do all this within these years? Others saw the zeal and love I have for the work and it made them join me. No man would want to join a directionless train. You can only remain in the anointing when you grow in it. This would be seen as Jesus concludes His instruction to Peter – John 21:19 ESV: ... *And after saying this he said to him, 'Follow me.'* Anyone who must remain connected to the Order must follow Jesus. Elisha followed Elijah and started acting the moment he received the mantle and that was what sustains it. The more you act in the anointing the more you seek the face of God.

Why sometimes we don't hear from God is because we have set idols in our hearts, which now form the basis for the prayers we say before Him which are centred on wants: '*Son of man, these men have set up idols in their hearts and put wicked stumbling blocks before their faces. Should I let them inquire of me at all? Therefore speak to them and tell them, 'This is what the Sovereign Lord says: When any Israelite sets up idols in his heart and puts a wicked stumbling block before his face and then goes to a prophet, I the Lord will answer him myself in keeping with his great idolatry. I will do this to recapture the hearts of the people of Israel, who have all deserted me for their idols*' - Ezekiel 14: 3-5 (NIV).

Does this declaration from God ring a bell as to why the world seems to be experiencing pains? We would say that the above scripture imply that God punishes those who desert Him for their idols and sets them as examples before all those who had gone astray. I don't expect anyone to prefer being set as an example of the burning fire of God's wrath. The Lord spoke to me on the 5th of August 2012, at around 11:50pm that the level of sin in the world is increasing and that the way to know is from the multitude of people seeking miracles these days from prophets because their hearts are far away from Him. The Bible says that righteousness exalts a nation, but sin is a reproach. The question now is who will preach to them so that they will desist from sins and become free. The more they sin, the more they rush for miracles as a means of alleviating the pains of their idolatry. This is the reason they are not receiving their desires. Many are being punished and their burden is increasing because they have not repented. Even as I teach the word in our church, I see these people running from pillar to post, not willing to repent, but hoping that one day they would receive their heart desires which is often to make more money in business or get cured – can any prophet or servant of God cure whom God has accursed? I don't believe. Their freedom is in their repentance.

The word of God also says: '*Son of man, if a country sins against me by being unfaithful and I stretch out my hand against it to cut off its food supply and send famine upon it and kill its men and their animals, even if these three men-Noah, Daniel and Job-were in it, they could save only themselves by their righteousness, declares the Sovereign Lord. As surely as I live, declares the Sovereign Lord, even if Noah, Daniel and Job were in it, they could save neither son nor daughter. They would save only themselves by their righteousness* – Ezekiel 14:13-14, 20.

The more I study scriptures and hear God speaking to me, the more I see the need for repentance rather than people running after miracles. In the days of Jesus, it was unrepentance that made Him to curse the lands where He had healed people, as they went back into sin. While the Anointed can intercede, the people need to know that without them turning away from sins, their burden will ever remain with them.

The Bible says that the disciples fellowshipped together,

breaking bread and drinking the wine of the communion, remaining faithful to the apostles' doctrine. We would see that even when you are trained in a particular profession, if you fail to employ the knowledge you have gained, after some time you discover that you could hardly remember anything, and you may become unproductive. The anointing grows through spiritual exercise – fasting, praying, employing the spiritual gift in solving problems, studying of the Bible, fellowship with brethren, evangelism, etc. This is why Jesus says the anointing flows like living water – not dead water, but water full of life. The negligence of growth in the things of the Lord was what made the Israelites to hew broken cistern for themselves which holds no water – Jeremiah 2:13.

Jesus told us the negative impact of not employing the anointing when he spoke to Peter – John 21:15 ESV: *When they had finished breakfast, Jesus said to Simon Peter, 'Simon, son of John, do you love me more than these?' He said to him, 'Yes, Lord; you know that I love you.' He said to him, 'Feed my lambs.'* The anointing is to feed others with the wisdom from heaven through teaching, and acts that will showcase the power of God. And from that same verse one would see that one of the things that would derail us from growing in the anointing is the love for the world. This is why He asked Peter: *do you love me more than these?'*

In the following discussion we outline the areas of growth,

learning from Jesus. The book of Luke 2:40,52 says of Jesus: 'And the Child (Jesus) grew and became strong in spirit, filled with wisdom; and the grace of God was upon Him. And Jesus increased in wisdom and stature, and in favour with God and men.' From these two verses Luke captured the areas which Jesus grew and any one desiring to remain relevant in the anointing from the Anointing Order must grow in these spiritual areas. Let's explain them in turn:

He grew and increases to become perfect as God with the following evidence:

1. **Strong in Spirit:** The use of the word 'Strong' shows that spiritual maturity is a growing process. The lack of this understanding is the reason why those who claimed to have received Christ fall into sin when they fail to grow spiritually through deep study of their Bible to improve personal fellowship with God. We would get a better insight in Proverbs 9:10: *The fear of the Lord is the beginning of wisdom: and the knowledge of the holy is understanding.* Anyone desiring the wisdom to live should start by obeying every command of the Lord and then have a perfect knowledge of God so that the meditation of his/her heart will be 'understanding' (Psalms 49:3). I still remember when God call me; there was no verse of the Bible I could quote offhand. But my walk with the

Lord has seen me through four years. The revelations I am having now are deeper than what I used to have in my earlier years. We grow strong in spirit when we seek Him daily and not relying on our own strength.

2. **Filled with Wisdom:** He grew and became filled with wisdom. A look at how He often referred to the scripture verses of the Old Testament shows that He studied, and understood what the prophets wrote concerning Him. Seeking wisdom is possible through zealousness.

3. **Grace of God upon Him:** Without the grace of God there is no way we can grow in His knowledge. This was why He made St. Paul to know that His grace was sufficient for him, so that he could do more exploits in the name of Jesus. When Jesus said that He has overcome the world, what He referred to was this abundant grace. But to enjoy this plentiful grace, we must have to employ our gifts in working in God's vineyard – wherever you find yourself, God expects that you display the attributes of the Order – to tender, and put things in perfect order.

4. **Mature in Stature:** This is only possible when one eats good nutritious food. Our physique stands out when we exercise. A study of the life of Jesus would tell us that He

wasn't the lazy type who would wait for others to work for Him while He slumbered. This would also be affirmed by the Bible verse which says: *Behold, He who keeps Israel shall neither slumber nor sleep.* We would also see that, 3 John 1:2, talks of the Anointed being in good health. This could be achieved through good food – avoiding junky food, avoiding drinking – alcohol or sugar-rich drinks, avoiding drugs, not sick from sexually-transmitted diseases, good personal hygiene, fasting, prayer, etc.

5. **Found Favour with God and Man:** The way we exercise our anointing tells how far we would grow in it. Having favour from God and man is only possible when we are delightsome. And this comes through the amount of value we attach to our gifts. We then need to employ every bit of the gift to ensure that we excel in all we do.

We see that through the help of the Holy Spirit which conceived Him He was able to grow to attain both physical and spiritual maturity, which made Him acceptable before God and man. During His ministry days, we found out how He would stay through the night sometimes in mount Olive communing with God. Those who grow in wisdom, knowledge and understanding which are the noticeable evidence of the Order's anointing must desire to grow by spending time with the source of these. Jesus gave us the clue to His strength below:

- **The Holy Spirit**: He proceeds from God, the father, to put things right in our lives: *But the Helper, the Holy Spirit, whom the Father will send in My name, He will teach you all things... -* John 14:26.

- **The Word:** The word of God carries the spirit of God, which is the intentions of the Melchizedek Order and anyone who would grow with these words will tend towards becoming a 'Melchizedian.' The Bible says: *The entrance of Your words gives light; it gives understanding to the simple. -* Psalms 119:130

- **Looking unto Jesus:** Jesus endured the cross and confirmed that He has overcome the world through the word He had spoken to His disciples (John 15:3, 16:33). This is why we must trust in Jesus and follow His ways:

- **Fellowship:** When we fellowship together in the courtyard of God, we mature together, through the helping hand of the knowledge we share. As the Bible says: *Iron sharpens iron, and one man sharpens another –* Proverbs 27:17 ESV

- **Serving in the vineyard:** Jesus told us that we must serve in the Lord's vineyard to be rewarded by the Order. Our continuous service will enable the Order to release information that will enable us mature and become relevant to society and the church.

The desire to grow our anointing should be strong in us, knowing that the more we grow in the anointing, the more influence we would have in every aspect of our lives, because we also grow in the wisdom to make decisions – leadership, administrative, and in our social lives.

Our anointing grows in stages. King David was Anointed three times and each time he became more influential than before:

1. David Anointed in the presence of his brothers: *Then Samuel took the horn of oil and Anointed him in the midst of his brothers. And the Spirit of the Lord rushed upon David from that day forward.* -1 Samuel 16:13 ESV

2. David Anointed as king over the house of Judah: *And the men of Judah came, and there they Anointed David king over the house of Judah.* - 2 Samuel 2:4ESV. This anointing gave him a wider scope of operation and administration than the one he had received in the midst of his brethren, but that anointing sets the pace for this one.

1. David Anointed as king over the whole house of Israel: *So all the elders of Israel came to the king at Hebron, and King David made a covenant with them at Hebron before the Lord, and they Anointed David king over Israel. David was thirty years old when he began to reign, and he reigned forty years. -* 2 Samuel 5:3-4ESV. This later honour was made possible because of his earlier exploits. Once Anointed he defeated Goliath, then he fought more wars and God gave him victory, which was what made him King over Israel. If you would employ your anointing, you will smile sooner than you expected.

And each time the anointing increases, the arm of the Lord was seen with greater power defending David, even against the house of Saul: *There was a long war between the house of Saul and the house of David. And David grew stronger and stronger, while the house of Saul became weaker and weaker.* – 2 Samuel 3:1ESV

People are looking for God and if you will carry His anointing, which is a seal of announcement from the Order, these same people will look for you to honour you. The secret is that you need to possess what people are looking to get from God, and they will come for you.

If you want to succeed in life, it is time you desired the anointing from the Order of Melchizedek. You will see your career and investments maturing before your very eyes. The anointing is all you need to overcome every burden and yoke of suffering in life: '*And it shall come to pass in that day, that his burden shall be taken away from off thy shoulder, and his yoke from off thy neck, and the yoke shall be destroyed because of the anointing.*' - Isaiah 10:27.

CHAPTER
TWENTY FOUR

INSIGHTS AND WISDOM

I will now be discussing some scripture verses which I call insights, and for each of these portions quoted, I will be bringing out the wisdom in them which we can take to heart and relate them to our path of success in life. The book of 2 Timothy 3:16-17 says: *All scripture is given by inspiration of God, and is profitable for doctrine, for reproof, for correction, for instruction in righteousness: That the man of God may be perfect, thoroughly furnished unto all good works.* This is why everyone who seek perfection and the anointing must be ready to study the Bible and receive spiritual illumination and insights from the verses the book contains to enable God approve us as one with sound doctrinal maturity – 2 Timothy 2:15.

The answer to your prayers is hidden in the verses of the Bible around you, with wealth in wisdom and knowledge on how to seek the strength you need to succeed in life. The Bible contains hidden wisdom and you are required to bring out this wisdom so as to affect your life positively. The more you study your Bible, the more the Melchizedek Order draws nearer to you. And your song shall be; Nearer my God, to Thee. Before we proceed with this discussion, let us sing the hymn – Nearer, My God, to Thee, Nearer to Thee! - Text: *Sarah Flower Adams, 1805-1848.*

Nearer, my God, to thee, nearer to thee!
E'en though it be a cross that raiseth me,
Still all my song shall be,
Nearer, my God, to thee;
Nearer, my God, to thee, nearer to thee!

Though like the wanderer, the sun gone down,
Darkness be over me, my rest a stone;
Yet in my dreams I'd be
Nearer, my God, to thee;
Nearer, my God, to thee, nearer to thee!

There let the way appear, steps unto heaven;
All that thou sendest me, in mercy given;
Angels to beckon me
Nearer, my God, to thee;
Nearer, my God, to thee, nearer to thee!

Then, with my waking thoughts bright with thy praise,

Out of my stony griefs Bethel I'll raise;
So by my woes to be
Nearer, my God, to thee;
Nearer, my God, to thee, nearer to thee!

Or if, on joyful wing cleaving the sky,
Sun, moon, and stars forgot, upward I fly,
Still all my song shall be,
Nearer, my God, to thee;
Nearer, my God, to thee, nearer to thee!

'Nearer, My God, to Thee' - by Sarah Flower Adams, a 19th century Christian hymn, inspired by Genesis 28:11–19, on the story of Jacob's dream, seeing a ladder connecting from the earth to Heaven and angels walking up and down on it. Later Jesus says that He was that Ladder that will take us to Heaven.

This is what we shall be doing in the following discussion. As we quote the insights from the Bible, we would extract the wisdom in them so that we can walk the path of righteousness in all that we do on earth, until that great day. And after reading through what we discuss here, I encourage you to use the same principle to study other insights in the Bible. All the verses quoted below are taken from the New Living Translation (NLT).

■ **Romans 6:1-2:**

Well then, should we keep on sinning so that God can show us more and more of his wonderful grace? Of course not! Since we have died to sin, how can we continue to live in it?

Wisdom: There is always a need to take a resolute decision not to commit sins again. Also, in our day-to-day engagements we often make mistakes which have made it difficult for us to climb to the height of success. What we need to do is to outline our mistakes and the reasons behind them, and then we may take the learning and move forward, with a frantic effort not to repeat them again. We can live a sinless life. We can also try to live a life of no mistakes.

■ **Proverbs 2:3-4**

Cry out for insight, and ask for understanding. Search for them as you would for silver; seek them like hidden treasures.

Wisdom: Knowledge abides everywhere the head turns. There is a saying that 'knowledge is power.' The success we envisage in life is hidden in someone's testimony and these testimonies are often written in books as stories, histories, or rendered as wise sayings. When we come across these, all we should do is take out the salient meanings and see how they would help us to succeed in life. The verses of the Bible are also very important and they are facts that explain what God desires are and how we can live to please him. Learn a trade.

Read books relating to the gift you have and discipline yourself to grow as you discover more hidden secrets that will make you do things easier than you have been doing. The Bible also says in Proverbs 3:13, 14: *Joyful is the person who finds wisdom, the one who gains understanding. For wisdom is more profitable than silver, and her wages are better than gold.* And also in Proverbs 8:10, 11 it says: *Choose my instruction rather than silver, and knowledge rather than pure gold. For wisdom is far more valuable than rubies. Nothing you desire can compare with it.* The more you receive wisdom concerning what you do, the more you become confident in pursuing your career and grow to maturity in the exercising of the gift you possess. A person with sound wisdom is one who fears God - Proverbs 9:10: *Fear of the Lord is the foundation of wisdom. Knowledge of the Holy One results in good judgment.* And this will help you live an upright life so that you will not experience pains in life - Proverbs 15:16: *Better to have little, with fear for the Lord, than to have great treasure and inner turmoil.* We are also advised in Proverbs 16:8: *Better to have little, with godliness, than to be rich and dishonest.* This is what knowledge does to us. When we are equipped with these kind of knowledge, there is no way we would succumb to pressures from other people trying to make us take decisions that will deface our integrity as we live and make a living.

■ **Proverbs 17:16**

It is senseless to pay tuition to educate a fool, since he has no heart for learning.

Wisdom: Learning is about desire. What you don't desire you don't get, because you will not be ready to endure the pains you may come across as you move on. Jesus had to endure the Cross to bring us salvation. What are you enduring to bring joy to your family, church and society? Everything we do involves learning, whether formal or informal. We receive learning as we encounter people and processes daily. What are you learning today and how does this learning add value to your gift and career in life? The only way you would know what to learn and what to jettison is when you have a plan and purpose for the life you would want to live. Everything involves planning. As you plan, you know what it takes to get you to where you are going. The heart to learn is the heart to endure, assimilate, digest, and regurgitate. Many also find it difficult to spend their money in buying books to read. You need to invest in books. What you don't buy, you can't take ownership of. You can't mark out important areas in someone else's book but you can on your own. Later you can go back and get better insight if the book belongs to you. Spend that money for knowledge and that knowledge will feed you someday.

■ Proverbs 6:6-8

Take a lesson from the ants, you lazybones. Learn from their ways and become wise! Though they have no prince or governor or ruler to make them work, they labor hard all summer, gathering food for the winter.

Wisdom: I have actually sat down to study the ants I see in my vicinity. And what I found out was amazing – how these little creatures understand the beauty of division of labour, defence, unity, hard work, resource management, hierarchical leadership and organization, etc. As I write this words, in the early hours of the day, I could hear young people shouting, sitting down and idly watching football. And sometimes when I see such things, including people just travelling to and fro, like the devil, without cogent reason, I often think I may be abnormal because every second matters to me. And I wouldn't want to waste any. The Bible says: *Indeed, he who watches over Israel, never slumbers or sleeps* – Psalms 121:4. Also Proverbs 6:10, 11 says: *A little extra sleep, a little more slumber, a little folding of the hands to rest—then poverty will pounce on you like a bandit; scarcity will attack you like an armed robber.* And we would also see in Proverbs 10:4-5 that: *Lazy people are soon poor; hard workers get rich. A wise youth harvests in the summer, but one who sleeps during harvest is a disgrace.* The beauty of planning is what distinguishes the ants. They know when to gather and when to build - Proverbs 21:5: *Good planning and hard work lead to prosperity, but hasty shortcuts lead to poverty.*

■ **Proverbs 12:11**

A hard worker has plenty of food, but a person who chases fantasies has no sense.

Wisdom: What are you chasing after today? Are you chasing after fantasies? The Bible says that anyone who does so is foolish. What are fantasies? There is an idiom I often take to heart – 'living in a fool's paradise', which means to be happy because you do not know or will not accept how bad a situation really is. Those who chase after fantasies are not truthful to themselves about the life they live. They are always seen playing about and wasting precious time. I always advise people that if they have nothing to do, they should go out to preach the gospel to somebody. Invest every second. Time and tide wait for no man. Many live a life of shadows with no concrete results for the years they have stayed on earth. The Bible says - Proverbs 21:17: *Those who love pleasure become poor; those who love wine and luxury will never be rich.*

I have seen many who waste resources with no viable reason for engaging in such wastage. In some cases, weddings and burials are too expensive. People waste money that would have been used in investment in buying outrageously expensive cars and houses. Now the Bible verse we are discussing talks about someone who is hard work. There are people who are hard workers but lack the wisdom that will help them plan ahead of the harvest. What beautifies hard work is the wisdom to plan your harvest and the knowledge to invest them, then your table will be filled with plenty food to eat always, and you will have enough to give out. This is wisdom. Other verses that buttresses what we have said include: Proverbs 13:4 - *Lazy people want much but get little, but those who work hard will prosper.* And Proverbs 13:11 - *Wealth from get-rich-quick schemes quickly disappears; wealth from hard work grows over time.*

■ **Proverbs 14:23**

Work brings profit, but mere talk leads to poverty!

Wisdom: The Bible says that we should be doers and not hearers alone (James 1:22). It is time for action. I have seen many people who have planned their lives and locked it up in their table drawers. When we receive wisdom, we should work with them in such a way as to add beauty to the life we live. Many people don't feel like investing their time to work out their plans because of the challenges they foresee. The more mature you become in knowledge and understanding, the more quiet and confident you become. What is understanding? – It is the value that the knowledge adds to your living. It is your ability to bring out the active statements or what I will call, 'the assignments contained in the knowledge you have received.'

■ **Proverbs 13:23**

A poor person's farm may produce much food, but injustice sweeps it all away.

Wisdom: Many people take what belongs to other people, especially the poor and needy. Anyone who does that will not see increase in life. This is because the Lord God Almighty will defend their case when they cry to Him. Cheating and swindling other people will only make us heap pains for our unborn generations. Those who undo the poor make them poorer and thereby mock God - Proverbs 17:5: *Those who mock the poor insult their Maker; those who rejoice at the misfortune of others will be punished.* We already know that many who are rich always think that the wealth is all that would sustain them without given a thought to their creator – Proverbs 18:11: *The rich think of their wealth as a strong defense; they imagine it to be a high wall of safety.* The more we do this, the poorer and more arrogant we would become because the Anointing Order would then withhold the Lord's blessings from us. We should therefore be guided as we employ our Anointed gifts to earn a living so that we would not cheat others.

■ **Proverbs 18:23**

The poor plead for mercy; the rich answer with insults.

Wisdom: Pride is the reason why a person would not plead for mercy when he/she is aware of the wrong he/she has done.

When we become arrogant, we also begin to build enemies who would obstruct our vision and growth in life. These become thorns and thistles growing in our vineyard. A look into the attributes of godliness as found throughout the Bible would showcase the value system of those Anointed. Many who have wonderful gifts of exploits have lived a life of shame and hopelessness because of pride and arrogance. Many who would have rendered help to them have avoided them because of their unhealthy and unwelcoming characters. If we would imbibe the advice in Proverbs 22:2 - *The rich and poor have this in common: The Lord made them both*, we would learn to treat everyone with respect and accord them due diligence in our relationship with them.

■ **Proverbs 28:3**

A poor person who oppresses the poor is like a pounding rain that destroys the crops.

Wisdom: I see this insight from the point of view of Christian brethren oppressing fellow brethren. Where will it land the church? Destruction! This is a fact we must learn as we grow in life. Are we destroying others' vision? To give a critique is value addition, especially when you tell it to the person involved. But to criticize is image damaging. And this is what is tearing homes apart today. The church can no longer exist as a family because of characters of this sort. What we should do is how we would be able to help one another, and projecting their good sides while advising them on their ugly side so that they would improve and yield more fruits.

■ Proverbs 3:5, 6

Trust in the Lord with all your heart; do not depend on your own understanding. Seek his will in all you do, and he will show you which path to take.

Wisdom: I have seen people die like fowl because their pride took them out of God's presence. Anyone who wants to live long and enjoy increase is one who surrenders his/her thoughts and decisions to God so that He would direct their path. When God speaks to us, there is no way we would make mistakes. The more mistakes we make, the poorer we become. And people will start avoiding us over our incessant mistakes.

■ Proverbs 30:7-9

O God, I beg two favors from you; let me have them before I die. First, help me never to tell a lie. Second, give me neither poverty nor riches! Give me just enough to satisfy my needs. For if I grow rich, I may deny you and say, 'Who is the Lord?' And if I am too poor, I may steal and thus insult God's holy name.

Wisdom: Prayers should be tailored to what you desire and what you know you have the heart to handle. This is the wisdom I learned from this prayer point. Many of us pray without asking ourselves if we would be able to handle what will result, peradventure the prayers are answered by God. This is why I see a prayer point as a project which must have a start and finish date. We should not wait until God answers our prayers before we would start putting things in place. Such rush may make us lose the beauty of what we had asked for. Only bite what you can chew at a time.

■ Proverbs 3:27

Do not withhold good from those who deserve it when it's in your power to help them.

Wisdom: This is an important instruction to anyone who would want to deny people their merited benefits and entitlements. Treat people who merit your favour, as the case may be, kindly. Give their reward to them as when due them, and in an appropriate manner. Do not rob Peter to pay Paul because Peter is your enemy. We are all equal before God. If you must excel in life, then respect people's entitlements and God will not withhold yours from you.

Now that you have read through the wisdom posited by this book, I would encourage you to take a trip into the world of the Bible, and prayerfully seek the help of the Holy Spirit, to open your understanding and then you would be able to bring out more wisdom from the verses you will come across daily to better your life and that of other believers.

May the Lord of host, who reigns from the Melchizedek Order fill you with the anointing that will announce you and all you lay your hands on– your testimony is the next. It is time to celebrate!

Good bye!

EPILOGUE

Humans, by default are sinful, being born into sin as a result of the adamic nature we bear at birth tainting our God-given gifts. It is the presence of the anointing in our lives that cleanses us from sin, so that we won't bear the burden of sin which is the reason why many of us fail in life. Once God is pleased with us, the Order follows us wherever we go and we experience His presence always, as someone within the coverage of a radar, until we are back again into His house: *Therefore say: 'This is what the Sovereign Lord says: Although I sent them far away among the nations and scattered them among the countries, yet for a little while I have been a sanctuary for them in the countries where they have gone.' ... I will gather you from the nations and bring you back from the countries where you have been scattered, and I will give you back the land of Israel again.'* – Ezekiel 11:16-17 (NIV).

Why would God take them back to Israel? It is because His temple is there. This gives us the understanding that when the Lord raises a servant who will work with the Anointing Order, and we join hands with him, to honour God by building a sanctuary dedicated for His service, His angels would move from the sanctuary, which is now like an extension of the Order, to follow everyone who worships in that sanctuary and everyone connected to Him would have the opportunity of functioning in the same anointing that is upon the servant of God. The protection and ministering from the angels is for a little while, which goes as far as we are still holy and righteous, which is why we always ensure we meet again and again, in His sanctuary to fellowship together and continue in the doctrine of Christ and the breaking of the bread and wine of the new covenant in our midst so that we would have a pure heart devoid of sin, the only ingredient needed in us to be able to see God.

You have heard of the anointing. You have read about it in Christian books as I have done. But the fact remains that the anointing has been treated as though it was some kind of power meant only for those who are pastors or preachers. As one called into ministry, I have come to discover with what God is doing in my life that the anointing lives in us right from that day when God breathed into Adam and he became a living soul.

Sin of disobedience is what affects the power of the anointing. Jesus says in John 10:10, that with the anointing we would live life more abundantly. All we need now is how to activate this anointing in us so that we would hear what the spirit says as we listen to anointed servants of God teach, as we sing and praise God in the beauty of His holiness, and as we live according to His commandments. This is the fact. So, God created you with a measure of the anointing which keeps you alive as we would infer from the life of Prophet Jeremiah - Jeremiah 1:5. All you need now is to grow it as someone on training as we did from our elementary class to the tertiary institution before we could boastfully seek a job. The Bible tells us of how Jesus grew His own anointing - Luke 2:40, 52.

The anointing thrives with the word of God. Sin shrinks it and it becomes dormant in us. But the more we receive wisdom and insight; the more it rejuvenates into a spring of living waters. What I see as born again is not someone speaking in tongues but someone who has a renewed mind, knowing that old things have passed away after coming in contact with 'Christine' wisdom - 1 Corinthians 1:24. Jesus wasn't expecting Nicodemus to speak in tongues; rather, He wanted Nicodemus to appreciate the fact that he needed to turn over a new leaf and appreciate what God was doing in this new dispensation of not being under the bondage of sin.

Many who speak in tongues these days do so to convince people that they have been born again. The act of tongues speaking was to enable preachers to break the barriers that language differences posses to good neighbourliness and to help them pray with the language of angels, not the reason why one will enter into heaven. Americans and many

Pentecostals the world over have spoken dozens of tongues from the Azusa street experience to date. Where is the world heading to today? The tongues we had spoken could not take gay marriage and crime off the street. We need wisdom and to teach same. This is what Christ meant in Matthew 28:20: *Teaching them to observe all things whatsoever I have commanded you.* This will enable us to add value to society. Christians need to wake up and seek wisdom from God so that our glory will not be turned into shame - Hosea 4:6-7, Jeremiah 8:9.

The disciples locked themselves up in Jerusalem speaking in tongues while Jesus had to raise St Paul to work for Him. God is busy raising novices daily and filling them with His word, while the acclaimed 'born-agains' are getting self-employed as prayer warriors, and frowning at every mark of success in other peoples' lives and attributing such successes to the devil. Tongues speaking without works is spiritual deadness. Many want the world to end now so that at last both the lazy, rich and the poor alike would go either to heaven or hell, as the disciples felt that Jesus came to restore Jerusalem so that they would enjoy good governance while the Gentile nations would languish in pain, and looking up to them as God's most favoured nation - but God don't think this way, He expects that we seek wisdom, live wisdom and teach wisdom, to those who will see the beauty of our works and repent - Matthew 5:16.

The solutions to our problems do not lie in miracles. I don't really advise people to seek miracles, because they make you always afraid of losing it, and your service to God will be marked with spiritual frights day and night. The Bible says that a nation is exalted through righteousness. Jesus healed so many and to some He commanded them to go and sin no more, and when they did not repent, He went back and cursed them - Matthew 11:21-24, whereas St. Paul had similar challenges but because he bears the Gospel in his lips, God says to him: 'my grace is sufficient for you' – 2 Corinthians 12:9. Which would you prefer - Miracles or preaching the gospel? The difference is in the fact that those referred to in Matthew 11:21-24 where lukewarm, without good works while St. Paul could show evidence of good works. The Bible says in James 2:18: *Yea, a man may say, Thou hast faith, and I have works: shew me thy faith without thy works, and I will shew thee my faith by my works.*

Jesus says the poor had the gospel preached to them. *Be wise!*

COVENANT CONFESSION

If you are not born again, you may have read this book as literary material and will not receive the spirit it carries. You can make a decision to correct that now by saying this covenant confession:

Lord Jesus, I know now that you died for my sins. I believe and confess you as my Lord and Saviour. Please come into my life and dwell inside of me.

If you just said this confession, you should locate a spirit filled church to fellowship with them – let the pastor know you just gave your life to Christ and you will be directed on what to do next. Salvation is a personal race and you must be serious with it.

You can also call us through the numbers below:

+234-8076190064; +234-8086737791.

Or send us an email at:

christmovementinternational@gmail.com

BOOKS BY THE SAME AUTHOR
1. Existing In The Supernatural
2. The Altar In Golgotha
3. How Good and Large is your Land?
4. Born To Blossom
5. Battles Beyond The Physical

6. The Path To Absolute Freedom
7. The Man God Made
8. Aspects of Marriage
9. Leadership – An Eagle-Eye Perspective
10. Gifted and Anointed

To contact Pastor Oghenethoja Umuteme, send an email to
president@christmovementinternational.org
You can join him on Facebook and Twitter also:
www.facebook.com/Pst Oghenethoja Umuteme
www.twitter.com/PstUmuteme

WORSHIP WITH US
@
ROYAL DIAMONDS INT'L CHURCH
(aka Christ Movement)
Nnata Close by Weli Street
Rumunduru/Eneka Road
Rumunduru
Port Harcourt, Nigeria
Please call or send us email to know our
worship days and time.
Phone: +234-8086737791
Email: christmovementinternational@gmail.com
info@christmovementinternational.org

ABOUT THE AUTHOR

Pastor Oghenethoja Umuteme encountered God the day he was baptised at the St Stephen's Anglican Church, Owhelogbo Delta State, when he received a warm feeling in his heart as he confessed the Lord Jesus as His lord and personal saviour. His birth was surrounded with mysteries – he was born to a mother who had been barren for 8 years. There was hardly anything he said that did not came to pass as he was growing. In 1994 he had a dream in which he received an orange which contained a bible with a red cover.

Events continued dramatically until he started hearing voices telling him to go for rescue, as many souls were heading for destruction. Then it became clear to him that he was being called to carry out the task of restoring mankind back to Jesus.

In January 2006, he heard a voice telling him to read Isaiah 42. On reading to verse 6, he felt a deep force within him and started trembling and a voice said - 'I have called you'. As he read further he was getting immersed in the spirit of God and when he read verse 22, the voice said, 'this is your task'.

Then on the 13th of October 2008, he heard a voice while driving: 'Service starts in your house on Sunday.' Events happened that were beyond his understanding and on

Sunday 19th October 2008, the first public worship service came to pass.

Pastor Oghenethoja Umuteme is a prolific writer. He is the Founder and Senior Pastor at Royal Diamonds International Church, Port Harcourt, Nigeria. He is an established teacher of the word of God and a prophet to the nation, as shown by his books. His wife, Mrs. Umuteme Adokiye Obele, has borne him two children, Elomezino and Aghoghomena.

www.ingramcontent.com/pod-product-compliance
Lightning Source LLC
LaVergne TN
LVHW011217080426
835509LV00005B/170